BEN GONZALES

SO-AVX-858

A

GUIDE   TO   TANZANIA

NATIONAL PARKS

A GUIDE TO TANZANIA NATIONAL PARKS

Lilla N. Lyogello

With a Foreword by Solomon ole Saibull

Travel Promotion Services Limited

DAR ES SALAAM

Travel Promotion Services Limited
P.O. Box 21703 Dar es Salaam

©Lilla N. Lyogello

Illustrations by: Peter P. Ndembo
Maps by: Costa Mahuwi

All rights reserved. No part of this publication
may be reproduced, stored in a **retrieval**
system or transmitted in any form or by
any means, electronic, mechanical, photocopying
or otherwise without prior permission of

the copyright owner

Cover designed by: Angela Adye
ISBN 9976 986 02 5

First published 1988

To Wildlife Managers and Naturalists; and to my wife and children

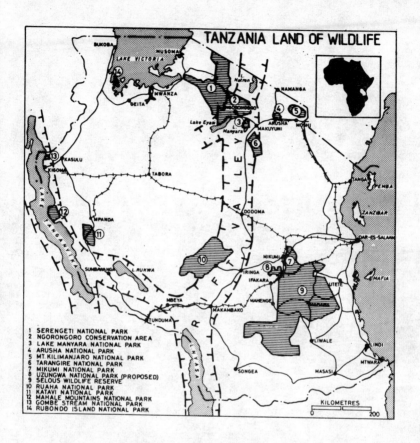

TANZANIA LAND OF WILDLIFE

1 SERENGETI NATIONAL PARK
2 NGORONGORO CONSERVATION AREA
3 LAKE MANYARA NATIONAL PARK
4 ARUSHA NATIONAL PARK
5 MT. KILIMANJARO NATIONAL PARK
6 TARANGIRE NATIONAL PARK
7 MIKUMI NATIONAL PARK
8 UZUNGWA NATIONAL PARK (PROPOSED)
9 SELOUS WILDLIFE RESERVE
10 RUAHA NATIONAL PARK
11 KATAVI NATIONAL PARK
12 MAHALE MOUNTAINS NATIONAL PARK
13 GOMBE STREAM NATIONAL PARK
14 RUBONDO ISLAND NATIONAL PARK

KILOMETRES
0   200

Tanzania......a country of striking differences — geographically, historically and
culturally. Nestled between the Indian Ocean and Lake Tanganyika, Tanzania
has more to offer to the world than other African countries. Incredible natural
beauty. A combination of the old and the new. Like medieval towns and
ultramodern hotels. As well as an endless variety of sports, beaches, national
parks, wildlife reserves, archaeological sites and festivals. It is unbelievable!

CONTENTS

MAPS, ILLUSTRATIONS AND CHARTS.

MAPS.

ILLUSTRATIONS.

CHARTS.

FOREWORD

by

Solomon ole Saibull

Former Minister for Natural Resources and Tourism, and Conservator of Ngorongoro

IN mid December 1984, a pleasant, friendly young man called in my office as I was about to go home. I had worked with him for a number of years when I was the Director of Tanzania National Parks. It was at this time he urged me to see his scripts on his proposed manual on national parks.

Next to me sat two other young men who asked me if I was planning to write a manual on Tanzania National Parks. I replied, "Oh no! But the man who should do such a manual is sitting here beside me — Lilla Lyogello.

Whether that was the moment when Lilla Lyogello first conceived the idea, I do not know, but we soon talked in a friendly atmosphere of such a manual.

Tanzania, unlike other African countries is blessed with an abundance of wildlife and natural beauty. Nowhere in the world can you see hundred of thousands of wild animals in their natural habitat as in Tanzania.

It is a wonder that anybody in the world should be proud of. It is in fact unique. But what was really needed was a manual — something that would give a visitor a reliable introduction to Tanzania National Parks and other wildlife areas such as Ngorongoro Conservation Area and Selous Wildlife Reserve.

Lilla Lyogello, a trained Wildlife Manager from the College of African Wildlife Management, Mweka in   Tanzania. was well qualified to do the project.

He has worked with Tanzania National Parks as a Park Warden-Tourism, in Serengeti for one year (1972) after which he was transferred to the Parks' Headquarters in Arusha to head the Public Relations Unit for six years (1973-78).

He then joined the tourist industry. To date he is working with the State Travel Service Ltd. as a Manager but he is very keen on Tanzania Parks. He is a very effective man in that wildlife forms part of the tourist products.

Lilla Lyogello has made it possible to describe briefly the parks, their major attractions and facilities. He has also included the names of Tour Operators and other useful information for visitors.

This manual therefore, is going to be useful not only to visitors, but to students at all levels.

Solomon ole Saibull
Arusha
December, 1987

PREFACE

THIS Manual is a guide to National Parks of Tanzania and its scope is epitomised in its title. It briefly covers all the Parks, Ngorongoro Conservation Area, the Selous Wildlife Reserve and the Marine protected areas.

It also gives useful information concerning some hotel/lodges and lists the names of some Tour Operators and other Organizations in the Tourist Industry.

The data upon which this Manual is based have been compiled from several sources. They are drawn primarily from the author's knowledge and experience, gathered when working with Tanzania National Parks; from information supplied by Wildlife Managers, and from a study of all the literature available on the subject.

I am especially indebted to Mr. B. Mbano, Mrs T. Boshe of the Wildlife College Mweka, for their constructive ideas; Messrs P.K. Ndilla of the State Travel Service Limited; and B.C. Mwasaga of Tanzania National Parks for going through and correcting my script; and to Mr. J.R. Kente, The Regional Game Warden (Arusha) for his valuable assistance.

It is this author's pleasure to record his deep appreciation and gratitude to the many persons — too many to mention individually — who have assisted in different ways.

I would particularly like to thank Miss Salma J. Tatakhan and Mrs Viorine Baguma, Mrs Joyce Lwambagaza and Miss Hidaya Seif for their great help in typing the script. Last but not least, I wish to record my gratitude to my wife, Monica Lilla, for encouraging me to write this Manual.

L.N. Lyogello

KEEPING ABREAST WITH CONSERVATION

MUCH has been written about 'conservation' in Tanzania. The term has become a household word to people who a few years ago were ignorant of both the word and its meaning. This is no wonder in this disturbed world, the natural habitats are quickly being destroyed through the increase of human population and civilizations accompanying demands upon the environment.

Only a few years ago people were much fewer than at present and their demands on the land were moderate. That is not the case now.

Man is aware that his way of life is increasingly defined by his surroundings. He knows that by destroying his land, he is on the other hand destroying himself. He is at the junction of the road where he has to choose either to live with nature, or do away with it. But if he selects the latter, it may be the end of him as well.

Tanzania's irreplaceable heritage — **wildlife** — has gained ground in popularity allover the world. Nowhere in the world can you see such abundance of wild animals in their teemingmillions as in the Serengeti and Selous for instance.

The Ngorongoro Crater, known geologically as a Caldera, is breathtaking. Tree climbing lions in Lake Manyara National Park are another wonder. Every park has combined features and animals of different species which can satisfy visitors of different levels and interests.

The Government and the people of the Republic are putting in every effort to ensure that the future generations may also see this resource. The former President of the United Republic of Tanzania, Mwalimu J.K. Nyerere, deserves many gold medals in nature conservation.

The establishment of **Malihai Clubs,** has further consolidated the firm foundation on conservationwhich has been laid. For it is the young men and women of today who will be the leaders of tomorrow, hence a great need to make them aware of their environment.

The formation of wildlife clubs alone is just one step in Nature Conservation. The government has to back up these clubs in all fields — manpower, money, equipment such as audio visual aids, transport, etc.

It is pleasing to note that the Ministry of Lands, Natural Resources and Tourism and the relevant bodies have taken up the matter seriously.

Experience from neighbouring countries which have well established Wildlife clubs has shown that through proper interpretation, conservation education from primary school to college level can play an important role both in preservation and conservation of the environment. As one conservationist put it: **'Through interpretation, understanding; through understanding, appreciation; and through appreciation, protection'.**

Records show that until recently the threat to conservation in most African countries was gaining an upper hand. This is now being reversed. Many countries have set up conservation units and a lot of money is being used for this purpose.

Very often a question arises as to why many governments are trying hard to conserve certain areas in a country. In short it is simply to protect nature from further destruction by human activities. It should also not be forgotten that certain environments are required for socio-economic reasons.

From the foregoing, therefore, it is not hard to see Tanzania's effort in this field. Apart from Wildlife and forest reserves — Tanzania has numerous controlled areas which are open to hunters only seasonally. This is between July and December of each year.

Through the Tanzania Wildlife Corporation whose duties include cropping, trapping of live animals and birds, tourist hunting, etc. the ecological balance of the various species has been maintained. It is for these reasons that the corporation employs trained and experienced professional hunters who know the behaviour of animals.

Tanzania boasts of eleven national parks. These are: Serengeti, Lake Manyara, Tarangire, Arusha, Kilimanjaro, Mikumi, Ruaha, Katavi, Gombe Stream, Rubondo Island and Mahale.

Strictly speaking Ngorongoro is not a National Park because, within it pastoralists have the right to **live and depasture** their cattle, goats and sheep. Also, Selous is not a National Park because hunting, however restricted, is permissible.

Within these parks, occupying slightly over 11 per cent of the total area of Tanzania, roam hundred of thousands of different species of animals. With the present efforts by the people and the Government, these resources of the last unexploited frontier may not be sealed off from their teeming millions.

Let us now briefly examine the history of each park.

SERENGETI NATIONAL PARK

SUMMARY

Establishment: 1951

Area: 14,763 Sq. km.

Location: Lies between latitudes 1° 28' and 3° 17' S and between longitudes 33° 50' and 35° 20' E.

Principal features: Short and long grass plains in the south; the *Acacia* savannah in the central area; the hilly more densely wooded area in the north; and the extensive woodland in the western corridor.

Altitude: 920 to 1,850m above sea level.

Major attractions: The Serengeti migration as well as lions; Kopjes and the open plains.

Best time to visit: December to February and May to July

Facilities: Lobo and Seronera lodges, camping sites, Youth hostel petrol station, garage and airstrips.

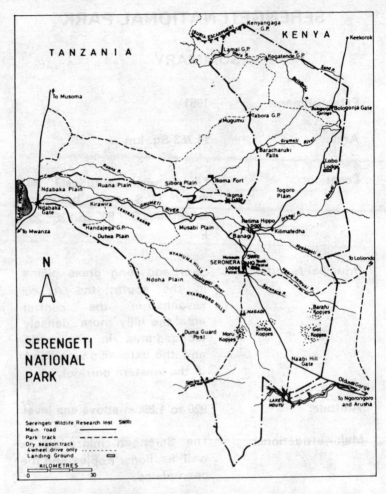

SERENGETI
NATIONAL
PARK

Serengeti Wildlife Research Inst SWRI
Main road
Park track
Dry season track
4 wheel drive only
Landing Ground

KILOMETRES
0   30

The Serengeti National Park is a thriller. With over three million large mammals, this park holds many pleasant memories: Of a variety of sounds at night, of a lion making a surprise kill late in the evening, but most of all memories of the "Serengeti migration."

SERENGETI NATIONAL PARK

The Park

THOUGH, millions of words have been written about the Serengeti National Park, they may be summed up in a few words only: "It is one of the most unique areas in the world"

Serengeti — a name that seems to conjure up all that is wildest in wildest Africa, was first protected in 1921.

Its Diamond Jubilee was celebrated in January 1981. (It was established as a National Park in 1951). It has an area of 14,763 sq km. and can be reached from Arusha at any time of the year. The park lies between **latitudes 1° 28'** and **3° 17'S** and between **longitudes 33° 50'** and **35° 20' E.** The name Serengeti is derived from the Maasai word "Siringet" which means "an extended area".

From Arusha one can drive South-westerly on a tarmac road for about 80 km., then branch off to the right at **Makuyuni** on an all weather murram road to Seronera in the heart of the Serengeti. A drive to Seronera. 335km. away from Arusha, may take six hours.

Apart from Selous, this park is the largest of all the parks in Tanzania. It lies between the Ngorongoro highlands and the northern Kenya-Tanzania border which form the boundary with the Maasai Mara Game Reserve of Kenya.

A corridor extends westwards to within 8 km. of the shores of Lake Victoria. An all weather road is planned to **Ndabaka Gate** which serves visitors from Mwanza or Musoma via Bunda.

Altitudes range from 920 to 1850 metres above sea level. Seronera, the park headquarters, is at 1530 metres. There were plans to scale down the headquarters in the interest of nature preservation and to relocate the main establishment of the Park at Mugumu in the periphery. It seems that these plans have now been dropped.

There is an all weather road which joins Seronera to Musoma via the **Ikoma Gate.** The same road branches at Ikizu and continues to Bunda and Mwanza to the west.

Musoma boasts of a modern Railway Hotel and visitors can cross the modern bridge at **Kirumi** on the Mara River to the Kenya-Tanzania customs post at Sirari via Tarime.

The principal features of the Serengeti Park are the short and long grass open plains in the south; the *Acacia* savannah in the central area; the hilly, more densely wooded northern section; and the extensive woodland and black clay plains dominated by the central ranges of mountains in the western corridor.

Throughout the whole park there is a variety of sceneries — plains, rivers, lakes, hills and rock outcrops, each of which has its own particular "atmospheric appeal" and range of wildlife; all these add to the fascinating variety of aestheticity

Major Attractions

The Serengeti Migration

One of the most breathtaking sights for visitors to the Serengeti National Park is the migration. Huge armies of nomadic animals move endlessly across the dry plains, furrowing the soil and its sparse vegetation with tens of thousands of trampling hooves.

The most outstanding features of the Serengeti is its **fauna**. It contains the greatest remaining concentration of plains game in Africa, and on a scale which has no parallel anywhere in the world.

This abundance of herbivores includes wildebeest, zebra, gazelle, topi, buffalo, hartebeest to mention but a few in an almost endless variety. Serengeti is also famous for its lions and contains a wide variety of birds-life-some slightly over 350 species.

But, the most spectacular and world famous sight has come to be known as the **Serengeti migration,** which usually takes place eastwards in November through January, depending on when the short rains start, and westwards in May at the end of the long rains.

The wildebeest migration in the Serengeti National Park is a continuous, all-year-round movement of slightly over 1.5 million animals. The main east-west trek is a twice yearly affair, but within these two streams are many mini-migrations.

In late May or early June, depending on the weather, the wildebeests move away from the short-grass plains between the Ngorongoro Highlands and Seronera and gradually disperse throughout the bush country to the north and west of the park where there is permanent water.

Here , they spend the next five months until triggered by the coming of the short rains in November, if early; they gradually form up into a number of columns and head back to the short-grass plains, thus completing the cycle. Calving takes place soon after arrival.

Many people, when referring to the migration in the Serengeti, have in mind the spectacular movements in November and at the end of May when the huge herds amass together for the start of their trek either east or north and west respectively. This is, certainly, a most wonderful sight.

Unfortunately it is very difficult to predict as it depends on such factors as the weather and the availability of water and grazing. In any case the main movement often lasts very few days and there may be a check caused by a sudden change in the weather, such as a heavy rain storm. Before the main exodus starts, however, the herds are a very spectacular sight, being massed in huge "armies" ready for the move.

At such times they are probably quite as photogenic as when actually on the march. It is at this time that rutting takes place westwards, and calving eastwards. The male animals patrolling and trying to maintain their harems of females as they trek westwards, and females delivering and practising their newborn calves in the art of survival by outrunning hyenas and wild dogs as they stampede eastwards.

Probably the best time to see the Serengeti wildebeest is from December through May when they are concentrated on the short grass plains in the south of the park. At this time they share the pasture with over 200,000 zebra and over half a million gazelle.

At the tail end of the procession come the cripple and those too weak to keep up with the rest, often falling victim to the inevitable following of lion, cheetah, hunting dog and hyena not to mention the vultures soaring overhead. Nevertheless, during the dry season when dispersed throughout the northern and western part of the park, the wildebeest are still a fine sight. At this time there is heavy concentration at watering places, and therefore more chance of seeing predators at work.

Vultures have an important biological role to play in the parks. These eagle — like birds with long wings are carrion feeders and can soar for long periods.

In a normal year the best time to see the concentration of wildebeest and other plains animals is during January and February when conditions are drier and a saloon car can be used. During the two periods of November December and March April May it may be essential for visitors to use a four-wheel drive vehicle.

It is worth noting that whereas the short-grass plains are the best for game viewing during the rainy season, the western corridor is more interesting during the dry months of June to October when, in any case, travelling is easier.

Facilities

There are two lodges managed by Tanzania Tourist Corporation: Seronera and Lobo Wildlife Lodges. Seronera Lodge is in the heart of the Serengeti National Park, approximately 145 km. from Ngorongoro Crater.

The lodge which consists of 75 self-contained double bedrooms is perfectly sited to command an excellent view of the annual migration of the animals through the Serengeti. There is also a dispensary, and a gift shop to cater for the visitors.

Seronera Lodge, like Lobo Lodge has been perfectly sited to command the Serengeti plains. The colour pattern, the design and the materials used to build it match very well with its landscape.

Lobo Wildlife Lodge is to the north of the park — close to the Kenya-Tanzania border. In a normal drive, it takes one and a half hours to get to Lobo from Seronera which is about 80 km. away. The lodge has been built into a great rock promontory with magnificent views of the Serengeti plains.

Like Seronera Lodge, Lobo Lodge has 75 self-contained double bedrooms. There is a swimming pool and a shop. And each of the two lodges has an airstrip. Lobo is a Maasai word meaning, **the place belonging to one man.** You have to be at Lobo in order to get the feel of one man's possession. The lodge gets its water from Lobo springs, about three kilometres away.

There are several camping sites around Seronera for visitors who do not want to stay in the lodge. A Youth Hostel is also present. Bookings for both camping sites and the Youth Hostel can be made directly at the Tourism Office at Seronera or at the Entrance Gate.

At the Tourism Office there is a petrol station while at the Park Headquarters there is a garage for vehicle maintenance and repair.

10

NGORONGORO CONSERVATION AREA

SUMMARY

Establishment: 1959

Area: 8,288 Sq. km.

Location: Lies between latitudes 2° 44'and 3° 26' S and between longitudes 35° 00' and 35° 55' E; and among lakes Natron, Eyasi and Manyara.

Principal features: Extensive plains, highland plateau, volcanic mountains, scenic craters and a superb forest.

Altitude: 1,350 to 3,600m above sea level.

Major attractions: The Ngorongoro Crater, the Empakaai Crater, the Oldoinyo Lengai mountain, the Olduvai gorge and the montane forest.

Best time to visit: December to February and May to July.

Facilities: Ngorongoro Crater, Ngorongoro Wildlife and Rhino lodges; Ndutu Camp, Landrovers, garage, petrol station, camping sites and an airstrip.

GORONGORO CONSERVATION AREA

The Area

MENTION the name *"Ngorongoro Crater"* to any nature lover who has been there, he will have no fine words to describe this "Africa's Garden of Eden". In short, it is breath-taking in its beauty.

The Ngorongoro Crater is about 190 kilometres west of Arusha, in the northern part of Tanzania. It is reached via the Arusha-Serengeti road in a spectacular three to four hours drive which takes the visitor to the base of the Great Rift Wall past the entrance to the Lake Manyara National Park and then to the Mbulu Plateau, past the Karatu wheat, maize and coffee farms, through the temperate forest up to **Heroes point** (2286m) at which the visitor first views the crater at the end of the ascent from **Lodoare Gate,** and finally along the Crater rim to the lodge.

The Ngorongoro Conservation Area covers an area of about 8,288 sq. km. of country embracing the volcanic highlands. It is situated

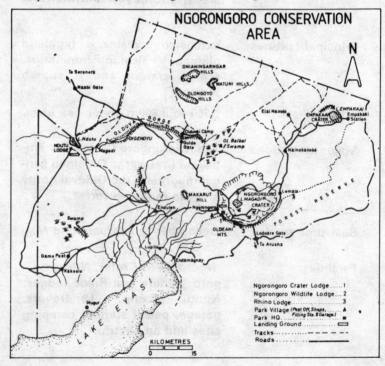

between **latitudes 2° 44'** and **3° 26' S** and between **longitudes 35° 00'** and **35° 55' E** and surrounded by three lakes namely Natron, Eyasi and Manyara. To the west it extends to include the eastern half of the Serengeti plains.

Formerly, the area was the core of the Serengeti National Park, containing its headquarters. However as a result of a human-wildlife conflict of interests, the park was divided to create the conservation area (1959) with a view to accommodate the grazing needs of Maasai pastoralists.

This area therefore, does not qualify as a national park so long as human interests of habitation and depasturage continue to be accommodated. Nevertheless, due to scrupulous restrictions on human activities, the area remains nature's paradise.

There are three groups of species co-existing: **Wildlife, Livestock and human beings.** These factors differentiate this area from other Parks wherein only wildlife is allowed to thrive. Farming is not allowed in any case. The Ngorongoro Conservation Area ranges in altitude from 1350 to 3600 metres above sea level.

The physical features include extensive plains, highland plateau, volcanic mountains, scenic craters, as well as a superb mountain forest which acts as a water reservoir for the surrounding farm country.

The conservation area derives its name from the famous Ngorongoro Crater — the sunken cap of an extinct but truly stupendous volcano which is regarded as one of the wonders of the world:

Major Attractions

The most striking feature in the Ngorongoro Conservation Area is the **Ngorongoro Crater,** of course. The first view of it, is absolute splendour. At Heroes point, there is a small rhino monument erected during the area's diamond jubilee celebrations, in January, 1981 in memory of fallen men in the service of conservation. After Heroes Point, there is a pillar on top of the graves of Professor B. Grzimek and Michael Grzimek, the world's outstanding naturalists and conservationists.

Professor Bernhard Grzimek, who died while watching a circus performance in Frankfurt, on 13th March, 1987 was buried on 26th May, 1987 beside the grave of his son, Michael, who died in a plane crash in 1959 while filming "Serengeti Shall Never Die", Never in the **history of conservation did Tanzania have such fine human beings. They were unbelievably remarkable.**

The crater has an area of 265 sq. km. and is 16 to 19 km across; the floor lies about 610m below the rim. Within the crater there are other attractive features. The lower reaches of the crater slopes carry sparse forests. In this regard, the Lerai forest on the crater floor, depends on ground water and the forest is dominated by the yellow bark tree, one of the *Acacias,* and a shrub fringe.

There is a shallow soda lake which sometimes remains dry, but there are springs and streams of fresh water for the animals to drink: There are also two swamps around two streams — the **Munge river,** and the Ol Chorronyokie.

Admittedly, the crater floor has beautiful grasslands which carry an estimated average of some 30,000 large mammals which include wildebeest and zebra, lion, hyena, rhino, cheetah, hippo, gazelle and baboon. This high concentration of resident animals is a tremendous spectacle.

The birdlife is also rich. Common birds to be seen are ostriches, Cape Crown Cranes, flamingoes, pelicans, Egyptian geese, eagles, starlings, etc. Some 350 species have been identified over a period of twenty five years since 1959.

Adult male lions with their attractive "mane" pause in the Ngorongoro Crater floor after a heavy meal. This "Africa's Garden of Eden — truly speaking — is the 'eighth wonder' of the world".

Just north of the Ngorongoro Crater, there is another small crater of significance. This is the **Empakaai Crater** which is known for its floral variety and exquisite scenic beauty. And not very far from this crater, there is the **Oldoinyo Lengai** (Mountain of God) as named by the Maasai. It is still an active volcano, and erupts every twelve to fifteen years. There was an eruption in 1966 and another one in 1979.

The **Olduvai Gorge** is another attraction of its own kind This is where the Leakey family discovered the remains of early man (*Homo habilis* and *Zinjanthropus boisei*) dating back to 1.7 million years. This significant discovery was made in 1959.

The Serengeti ecosystem includes the Ngorongoro Conservation Area, the Maswa Game Reserve and the Maasai Mara Game Reserve. Together they cover a total area of 40,350 sq. km. The area therefore, is of vital importance to the Serengeti ungulates and future well being in general.

The Ngorongoro highlands have beautiful **montane forests.** These act as a water-catchment area. Hence its great role in maintaining the water-regimes in the farm area surrounding it.

Facilities

The Ngorongoro Crater Lodge is one of the oldest, yet most up-to-date Game Lodges in East Africa. The earliest buildings date back to 1937. The latest — the log-style dining room and lounge, providing restaurant and bar facilities — was completed sometime in 1963. The lodge has about 134 beds and commands a superb view over the crater.

Future plans include building four executive suite rooms; installing telephone system in all the rooms and renovating the whole lodge. The lodge management also plans to increase its fleet of Landrovers and combis for safari.

The months of July/August through March are the busiest and visitors are advised to book accommodation well in advance. A deposit of not less than 50% for this is required.

The other lodge is the Ngorongoro Wildlife Lodge which became operational in 1969. It is situated on the rim of the crater at an altitude of 2286m above sea level. It is only 60 kilometres from Lake Manyara National Park. The lodge is of modern design, with 75 self contained double bedrooms all having a panoramic view of the crater.

All the bedrooms are centrally heated. This lodge belongs to the Tanzania Tourist Corporation (TTC). Reservations may be made through the State Travel Service Ltd. — Arusha or through TTC Reservations Office, Telex No. 42037 UTALII TZ.

There is another lodge run by the Ngorongoro Protection Fund under the auspices of the Ngorongoro Conservation Area Authority. This is the Rhino Lodge. The Lodge provides full board accommodation, indoor sanitation and hot water. There is a cosy bamboo bar.

The lodge is situated near the rim of the crater in a valley with a beautiful view. Animals can be seen from it in forest glades. The glades are often frequented by big game, such as buffalo, which can be seen at close quarters from the verandah.

Ndutu Tented Camp is situated about 90 kilometres from the Ngorongoro Crater. It is a very popular camp, especially during the migration. The camp which is at the boundary of the Serengeti National Park and the Ngorongoro Conservation Area provides full board accommodation. Apart from the lodges found in this area, the State Travel Service Limited maintains a fleet of Landrovers for crater tours. There is also a garage for vehicle maintenance.

The Ngorongoro Protection Fund also operates a smaller fleet of Landrovers for crater tours. Due to their demand, these must be booked well in advance.

The Ngorongoro Conservation Authority has a petrol station as well as having telephone and radio call communication with its Public Relations Office in Arusha and sub-stations in the area. A dispensary and tourist shops are also maintained in the area. There is an airstrip at the rim of the crater for charter planes.

And for campers, the Authority has camping sites at the rim of the crater, inside the crater and at Lake Ndutu. For the more adventuresome, camping on the rim of Empakaai Crater can be arranged, seasonal road condition permitting.

Camping is allowed in most parks. Such sites are very ideal to those who intend to have a feel of the wilderness — away from the hustle and bustle of the cities.

SAFARI INTO SPLENDOUR

MANY activities and animal incidents in our parks and wildlife reserves pass unrecorded. These areas are so vast that it is impossible to record and monitor all details in each area. The people who can record: Game and Park Wardens as well as rangers, cannot be every where at any one given time.

In mid June, 1984 I escorted a group of three tourists from the USA to Ngorongoro Crater, Serengeti and Lake Manyara. After meeting and introducing myself to the clients at the Kilimanjaro International Airport, we boarded the State Travel Service van and drove off to Ngorongoro. We arrived at this eighth wonder four hours later.

Our first home for the next two days was at the Ngorongoro Crater Lodge overlooking the crater. Unknown to all of us, it was from this place that our real excitement was to begin. The scenery of the caldera was a source of inspiration to the visitors. The topography and geological features were just too spectacular and nothing in the world could be comparable to this, my visitors told me.

Early the next morning we drove off in our Landrover to the floor of the bowl-shaped crater. We had to descend 610m through the meandering road in order to get there. Visibility was hindered by low clouds touching the ground, typical of high mountain country. However, I assured the visitors that it would be clear by the time we got down the crater. The cold weather made our safari a bit uneasy. At an altitude of 2286m above sea level, it could certainly be cold. We negotiated our way through the zig-zag road on the rim of the crater. It took us about forty minutes to get down to the floor of the crater, slightly over fifteen kilometres away.

Down the crater there was sunshine. The cloud we had passed through could now be viewed, marvelled at, and photographed from the warmth of the crater floor. The cotton-wool like cloud flowing down the walls of the crater appeared like an impressive waterfall.

Indeed the visitors were amazed at the whole set up. For it was here that the world really looked young and fragile, held in trust for all mankind.

Our first hosts to welcome us in the crater, were funny looking wildebeests. I had a busy day pointing out at the different types of animals found in the crater, for my clients had seen only a lion in a zoo.

They had not seen the other species of animals. I told them about trees, grasses, birds, soil types and what have you. They wondered how long it took to know all these things; "I was a trained Wildlife Officer by profession", I told them lightly.

We drove past the beautiful **Lerai Forest** in the hope of coming across a kill. There was nothing. We drove on and on, on the

18

gravelled and dusty road — only antelopes and hyenas were seen in abundance. When we were about to despair, we saw what we were looking for. A pride of lions was stalking a lone zebra. To avoid disturbance, I told the driver to stop immediately; for if he continued he would unset the trap.

Our hearts nearly skipped a beat in excitement. The hunters were the females. The males watched in amusement and hope as the three females formed an extended line and started to move towards the zebra. They stalked for about one minute. The hunters were at an advantage in that the grass which camouflaged them was reasonably tall and on the leeward direction of the wind.

The zebra could not therefore, sense any danger. As the lionesses were within a striking distance, they moved in like lightning. All what we saw was that one lioness was already "riding" on the back of the zebra and the other holding onto the neck and mouth. The third lion was on standby just in case.

At this juncture we drove to the scene to see at close range what was going on. The zebra struggled bravely but it could not free itself from these hungry beasts. As the zebra's strength ebbed away, the struggles became less and finally it conceded defeat and fell down. As usual the male lions came in and chased the females. It was the males which started to eat first and after they had filled their stomachs it was the turn of females to do the same: Lions have very chauvinist behaviour.

Survival in the wild means "to eat and not be eaten". These lions are having their supper after making a successful kill.

In attendance at this kill for the left-overs were other **predators and scavengers;** hyenas, jackals, vultures soaring above, and other birds of prey formed what one could be termed garbage collectors. They were very helpful animals; for apart from checking the numbers of herbivores, they help park management to keep the areas clean.

After some time we left that site with permanent memories of that unforgettable incident.

I had earlier on promised my clients about seeing rhinos in the crater. I knew of a certain area in the crater where it was possible to see these endangered animals. I explained to the visitors the natural history of the animal: A rhino could weigh anything up to one and a half tons; its eyesight was very poor, and could hardly see more than 30 metres away. It depended more on its sense of smell. The gestation period of the animal was pretty long, about 18 months. I further told my clients that a rhino was quite dangerous and that it could charge any moving object. So we drove on and after a few minutes our eagle-eyed driver, one arm on the steering wheel and the other pointing at an animal, broke the silence and shouted: "Rhino!"

As we approached the animal we noticed that, close to the mother there was a calf which looked hardly three weeks old. I turned to my clients and told them that such a rhino could be even more dangerous as it had a very young calf which needed great protection. The rhino which was feeding had now stopped.

It had heard the sound of a coming van. We were barely 40 metres when its head swung towards our direction. We were within 30 metres

Oh, what an experience! When it senses an intruder, a rhino will usually make a dummy charge, not always in the exact direction, in order to cause tell-tale movement which enables it to locate the enemy. This one seems to have located the cause of the disturbance; but such incidents are very rare in the parks.

before I realised that the rhino was now serious. We heard it panting like a steam engine up a grade. It thundered towards us, and using its long horn it knocked our landrover on the driver's side three times. It then turned back and ran away.

To my clients this was perhaps the most terrifying incident they had witnessed in the wild in their lifetime; to me it was a repetition of past events. I urged them to take pictures quickly before the animal was out of sight. They did so quietly and when the animal was out of the flight distance they looked at each other and laughed.

We left that place and decided to head to the north of the crater hoping to encounter more thrills. We scanned a good part of the area but encountered no incident. We then decided to return to the lodge and on the way back we saw yet another unforgettable event.

A lone buffalo was grazing by the road and about a hundred metres away from the main herd. Close to the lone buffalo were a dozen lions. Within seconds two daring lionesses started to stalk the buffalo.

Lions belong to the cat family and it is very interesting to see them hunting. As the hunters got nearer to their prey we realised that the buffalo was in trouble. All of a sudden we saw one lioness on the buffalo's back while the other was holding onto the flank. Buffaloes are very strong animals and a fully grown bull could weigh up to a ton. The prey was caught unaware but despite this short coming it struggled hard to save its life.

It charged furiously at these kings of the jungle. Suddenly it changed course and with its predators on the back, ran towards the herd of buffaloes. As the buffalo got nearer the herd, the lionesses sensed danger, and metaphorically abandoned ship. The lionesses looked disappointed as they rejoined the main pride of lions which seemed not to care about what was taking place.

We returned to the Crater Lodge safely. It took us a short time to get to the top as the road down is different from the road up. After a delicious breakfast the following morning, we left Ngorongoro Crater for Seronera in the Serengeti. The fog that had dominated the Ngorongoro Highlands gave way as we came out into the *Acacia* grassland plain. It became warmer and we had to put our jackets aside in order to compromise with the heat.

After a gruelling drive on that crazy road for about two hours, we finally reached the **Naabi Hill Gate,** the entrance to the Serengeti National Park from the east, and Ngorongoro's western exit. We paid our entrance fees and drove off.

The wildebeest and zebra which normally dominated the short grass plains during certain periods of the year were nowhere to be seen. It was the Thomson's gazelle which featured most in this area at that particular time. As we approached Seronera our vehicle grounded to a halt.

"Was it a breakdown again?" were our unspoken thoughts. But the driver seemed not to be worried at all. Instead of getting out to check the vehicle, he asked for a pair of binoculars. Over a kilometre away he had spotted a cheetah resting on an ant-hill. It was so far that only a trained and experienced eye could tell the type of animal by simply looking at its posture. We drove closer to the cheetah and to our surprise we noticed that the cheetah had three cubs. They were playing in the shallow den probably dug by hyenas.

Not very far from the cheetah there were Thomson's gazelles, a favourite prey for cheetah. The antelopes had sensed danger, for they were all looking in one direction — towards the cheetah.

We told our visitors to be patient and watch. The gazelles which were still within flight distance continued to gaze at the cheetah. As the latter continued to approach the astonished animals, some started to run away. Those which pretended to be bold stood firm on the ground; it was one of those which later on fell prey to the cheetah. Cheetahs are known for their speed and agility. It has been recorded that a cheetah could run up to 112km. per hour making it the fastest land mammal in the world!

As the hunt continued, we sat in our van to watch the tempo build. Leaving the cubs behind and moving tactfully, the cheetah spotted one gazelle in the herd which it could handle effectively. Without hesitating the cheetah made a solo move. It isolated the selected gazelle from the rest of the herd and sped after it. Moving on and on, with its tail, coiling and recoiling and after a few seconds we saw a cloud of dust.

Of all the animals of the African Savannah, the cheetah is without doubt the speed champion, capable of attaining 112 km per hour over short distances. Here, it is leading its prey to a nearby hideout where it will enjoy its meal peacefully.

22

We moved in closer to see what was happening. The cheetah had pawed the gazelle on its hind quarters and it was now holding tightly onto its throat; for that was the way cheetahs killed their preys - by suffocation. We realised that the cheetah was very tired However, it crouched and continued to hold onto its prey. It jumped off just as the gazelle fell down and died.

The cubs moved in to share the feast. The moderate wind that was blowing had all of a sudden ceased. Other gazelles were looking at this predator from a distance in disgust. All was quiet in this part of the world. Nature had really taken its course.

Unlike leopards, cheetahs do not have a habit of taking their prey up a tree; they eat on the ground. This exposed them to all sorts of interference. They were very vulnerable to other predators as such they had to eat their meal hurriedly and leave the left-overs to others. This cheetah with its cubs was not an exception; it fell in the same line just like other cheetahs.

We arrived at Seronera Wildlife Lodge in the afternoon. My visitors appreciated the architectural design of the lodge as well as its location. The lodge is built on and is surrounded by rocks making it match with the surroundings. From Seronera we went to the western corridor, past the **Ikoma Gate** in Sibora area to view the migration. This was on the second day.

The wildebeest and zebra were so many that only an aerial count would have given us an approximate figure. According to the population census carried out in Serengeti in 1978, it was estimated that there were **1.5 million** wildebeest alone. To-date, the number could certainly have gone up. It is indeed an amazing sight to be in the Serengeti during the migration. Apart from these ungulates, we also saw many lions and cheetahs, let alone hyenas.

"To be in the Serengeti especially at night and try to listen to the animal sounds was just like going to a music hall and listen to various music bands each playing a different song and tune" commented one visitor. It was on the following day when we left Seronera for Lake Manyara Hotel for an overnight stay there. We wound up our trip with a morning game drive the following day in the Manyara Park.

In this park my clients saw thousands of pelicans and other birds in the trees and in the lake. They also saw the famous tree climbing lions in the *Acacia* trees. After our lunch at Lake Manyara Hotel we sped towards Arusha where the visitors had their last night at the Mount Meru Hotel.

"Your country is so beautiful that what we had seen and experienced is contrary to what we heard at home. We can assure you that no country in the world can match Tanzania in terms of wildlife and beauty", they told me as they boarded their jet back home.

I thanked them for their kind words about this country; and with a smile I said "Kwaheri" and welcomed them once again to Tanzania, the Land of Kilimanjaro.

NOTES

24

LAKE MANYARA NATIONAL PARK

SUMMARY

Establishment: 1960

Area: 325 Sq. km.

Location: Situated between latitudes 3° 20′ and 3° 40′ S and longitude 35° 45′ E.

Principal features: Great Rift Valley, the lake and the Groundwater forest.

Altitude: 945m above sea level.

Major attractions: Tree climbing lions, elephants, birds, groundwater forest, hot springs and rift wall.

Best time to visit: December to February and May to July.

Facilities: Lake Manyara Hotel, camping sites, Youth hostel, garage and petrol stations.

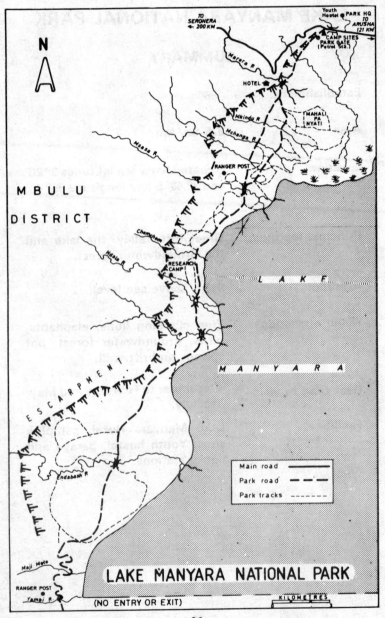

LAKE MANYARA NATIONAL PARK

LAKE MANYARA NATIONAL PARK

The Park

ABOUT 130 km. southwest of Arusha en route to the famous twin World Heritage Sites, Ngorongoro and Serengeti, lies another tourist attraction — the Lake Manyara National Park. It takes about two and a half hours to get there from Arusha. This park was established in 1960 and has a total area of 325 sq. km. of which 229 sq. km are the lake.

Lake Manyara National Park is within the Great Rift Valley which stretches from Turkey to the Zambezi, and follows the Red Sea, along the line of the Ethiopian Highlands through Sudan, Kenya, Tanzania and Malawi. Following the Rift Valley to Kenya, the fault divides into eastern and western arms. Manyara is within the eastern arm and is situated between **latitudes 3° 20′** and **3° 40′ S** and **longitude 35° 45′ E.** The altitude is about 945 metres above sea level.

Manyara is a Maasai word for a plant — emanyara — used for making living stockades around their kraals. It is scientifically called *Euphorbia tirucalli*. Other Maasai elders argue that it comes from the word Ol Manyara which means — settlement. The outstanding features of the Park include the spectacular escarpment of the Rift wall. The park also boasts of different habitats: *The Groundwater Forest* which can be seen immediately on entering the park covers an estimated area of 1300 hectares. It extends from the gate to Msasa River.

The dominant vegetation include: *Trichlia roka, Tabernaemontana usambarensis, Celtis zenkeri* and *Croton macrostachys*. This canopy vegetation contains shrubs, herbs and grasses which forms a good habitat for baboon, rhino, buffalo, crested guinea fowl, hornbill etc. One notable feature is that the forest is fed by permanent streams which gush out from the volcanic rocks below the rift wall. Adjacent to the Groundwater Forest, there is the *Acacia tortilis* woodland. This covers an area of 1820 hectares and extends from Msasa to Bagayo river.

As the name implies the dominant vegetation species is *Acacia tortilis*. There are also drought tolerant species such as *Balanites aegyptiaca, Salvadora persica, Cordia gharaf* as well as *Caparis tomentosa*. The vegetation is good both for grazers and browsers. Hence elephant, impala, buffalo and giraffe find this area to be their favourite ecological niche. From Endabash towards the southern end of the park can be found the *Mixed woodland* which covers an area of 2290 hectares. The vegetation in this area include *Acacia tortilis, Balanites aegyptiaca,* and *Kigelia aethiopica*. Others are *Caparis fascicularsis, Gardenia jovistonantus, Abutilon, Solanum, Tagetes* and *Ocimium*. This home range is ideal for elephant, rhino, impala, giraffe and zebra.

The *Alkaline grassland and glades* are located along the lakeshore and within the groundwater forest. The dominant vegetation species are the *Chloris gayana, Sporobolus spp, Cynodon dactylon* and *Bothrochloa radicans*. They provide grazing for the majority of the animals especially buffalo, wildebeest and zebra.

Lastly, the *Dry thicket or escarpment vegetation* is found along the escarpment. It consists of deciduous trees and thickets which for many years, have been modified by fire. The common trees include *Commiphora spp* and *Acacia spp* associated with *Lannea stulmanii* and *Sclerocarya birraea. Dalbergia melanoxyolon, Selonia elata* and *Fagara chalybea* are also common. Large baobabs, *Adansonia digitata* occur throughout. Elephants are common on the escarpment and are seen descending to the plains in the mornings.

Due to this variety of habitats, there are different species of animals and birds using these areas. The same habitat may be used by several species of animals at different times or levels. Thus a giraffe, rhino and gerenuk may use, say an *Acacia* plant at different levels. The average rainfall in the park is about 760mm. The long rainy season begins in March and continues through May. A heavy rainstorm sometimes may occur in April or May and this can cause temporary closure of some tracks in the park.

Major Attractions

Lake Manyara National Park is famous for **tree climbing lions.** Various reasons have been postulated as to why lions in this park

Having a siesta? Yes. Tree climbing lions are one of the major attractions in Lake Manyara National Park. Such sights can be encountered in the Acacia woodland.

spend much time resting in trees. Yet to-date no particular reason has been singled out as the determining factor for this habit. However the reasons include: to avoid the tormenting flies; to catch the breeze; to obtain a view; to find a spot cooler than the ground below or, most probably, to keep out of the way of the buffalo and elephant herds.

The most preferred trees by lions are *Acacia* trees. It is common therefore to see chicken mesh wires put around the main stem to prevent elephants from debarking and in the final analysis kill the trees. The National Park Management has a duty to preserve this habitat to prevent its total elimination. However, the future is not as bleak as it once appeared to be in the late sixties and early seventies. There is a healthy regeneration of the **Acacia** trees in the park. Manyara is also famous for its **concentration of elephants.** It is said that the highest density of elephant in Africa is at Lake Manyara National Park. There have been seven elephants to the square kilometre.

The dwindling giants on the march to an unknown destination. Each year, thousands of visitors come in flocks to see wildlife. Elephants are one of the so called "big five". The others are rhino, buffalo, lion and leopard.

There is a fantastic **profusion of birdlife** in Manyara. Over 380 species have been recorded in the park to-date, some of these only occurring seasonally.

The **groundwater** forest found around the gate is another attraction. Here, the tall trees are maintained by water which seeps out of the rift wall. In this forest there are three types of vegetation growing at three separate levels; canopy trees, shrubs, and grasses, including reeds, and other flowering plants.

Other animals which may be seen in abundance include: hippo buffalo, giraffe, baboon, wildebeest etc. One may include the hot springs in the south of the park as another attraction.

Facilities

Visitors to this park can be accommodated at the Lake Manyara Hotel which is a tourist hotel. The hotel has been built on the edge of the Rift wall and thus it commands the view of the Lake Manyara National Park below. One can view the park from the hotel by using a telescope built within the hotel premises. There is also a swimming pool as well as facilities for table tennis and darts.

At Kilimamoja, about a kilometre away from the Lake Manyara Hotel, that is at the turn-off to the hotel, and at the village of Mto wa Mbu (Mosquito Creek) eight kilometres away, there are several guest houses where visitors can be accommodated at relatively cheap price. The guest houses provide simple but clean rooms and it is practical to be armed with a mosquito repellent just in case the room is not mosquito proofed. At the village there is a petrol station and a market. Visitors — especially campers — can obtain their supplies from here. Fruits such as bananas, pawpaws, and green vegetables are available. There is also a wide selection of carvings, spears, batiks, etc.

The park has camping sites at the gate. One of them has bandas (huts) equipped with beds, cooking and eating utensils. These facilities can be hired at reasonable prices indeed. For people with limited funds or who want privacy this place is very ideal. Bookings may be made direct to the park. A Youth Hostel at the Park Headquarters can accommodate up to 48 people. There are beds in the hostel but all beddings have to be brought by the visitors, along with cooking and eating utensils.

There is also a garage at the Park Headquarters and visitors having problems with their vehicles may get them repaired here. A petrol station is also present at the gate.

TARANGIRE NATIONAL PARK

SUMMARY

Establishment: 1970

Area: 2,600 Sq. km.

Location: Situated at latitude 3° 50' S and longitude 36° 00' E at the centre

Principal features: The Tarangire river, nine vegetational zones, hills engulfing the park, swamps and rock outcrops.

Altitude: 1,100m above sea level.

Major attractions: *Acacia tortilis* parkland, tree climbing pythons, Tarangire river, landscape and swamps.

Best time to visit: September to December.

Facilities: Tarangire Safari camp, camping sites, airstrip.

TARANGIRE NATIONAL PARK

The Park

THE Tarangire National Park is situated in Northern Tanzania at **latitude 3° 50′ S** and **longitude 36° 00′ E** at the centre. Its name comes from the Tarangire River which rises in the Kondoa Highlands of Central Tanzania and makes its way north-wards through the length of the park. One arm forks to the right feeding the Nguselororobi and Larmakau areas; while the left hand one coils and coils, and finally pours its water into Lake Burungi. The river forms a dry season retreat for game, and although long stretches are devoid of surface water, enough pools remain to attract thirsty animals especially during the months from July to November.

Before becoming a national park, Tarangire was originally a popular hunting area. Today it is regarded as one of the best wildlife areas remaining in East Africa. The principal features of the park include the lake, swamps, rivers and rock outcrops. Interestingly, this area is engulfed by several hills: Oldonyo Ngahari is to the east while Kalima is to the south; Sangaiwe and Haidedonga are to the West and Kitibong a bit further inside' from the two. On the other hand Tarangire hill is almost centrally located.

The park management has developed some tour circuits to enable visitors to observe this miniature world at their own pace. Each circuit has its own outstanding features which can imprint into ones mind the thrill of a lifetime. Hence the tracks in the park are such that they enable one to visit all the circuits, namely; Lemiyon, Matete, Burungi, Kitibong, Gursi, Mkungunero, Nguselororobi and Larmakau.

The rainy season begins in November and continues through May. The highest precipitation may be recorded in March. However, the rainfall in the park is low, approximately 600mm. per annum. Tarangire covers an area of some 2,600 sq. km. and is sixth in size after Selous, Serengeti, Ruaha, Ngorongoro and Mikumi, in that descending order. It was opened in 1970.

There are nine distinct vegetational zones in the park each of which has its own atmospheric appeal. Most prominent is the *Acacia* Parkland which is characterised by scattered trees and is dominated by *Acacia tortilis*. This habitat is ideal for impala, giraffe, waterbuck, hartebeest and eland. The *Acacia — Commiphora* zone varies from open grassland to dense thicket. It is here where black rhino, lesser kudu and waterbuck can be sighted.

The other vegetational zone is the *Combretum — Dalbergia* woodland where zebra, eland and giraffe are common animals. Interestingly, the *Gall-Acacia* woodland constitutes a zone of *Acacia drepanolobium* dominants associated with tall grass featuring

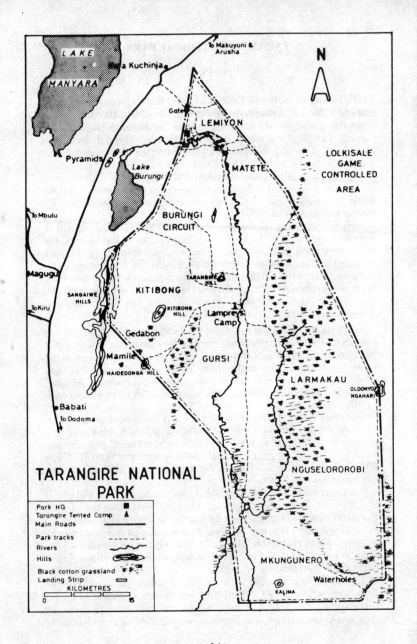

TARANGIRE NATIONAL PARK

Park HQ ■
Tarangire Tented Camp ▲
Main Roads ────
Park tracks ─ ─ ─
Rivers ∿∿∿
Hills ⬭
Black cotton grassland ⁂
Landing Strip ▭

KILOMETRES
0   15

waterbuck, impala, Grants gazelle and giraffe. Reedbuck and wildebeest may be encountered in the **Riverine Grassland** area where the vegetation consists of different plant species that include the tall elephant grass, reeds and *Acacia tortilis*.

Admittedly, the **Deep Gully Vegetation** with its steep walled riverines has a cool climate and supports relatively good growth of trees. Animals in this zone include elephant, rhino, leopard, hyena and buffalo. The **Drainage-line** woodland which supports palatable grasses and shady trees; and the **Open Grassland** with extensive flood plains, are the other zones. The grasses found here are tall and fast growing. Tree climbing pythons are normally found in this zone and buffalos use the area effectively. Lastly, there is the **Rocky-hill tops** consisting of stunted trees, bushes and shrubs. Klipspringer and rock hyrax are obvious inhabitants.

Major Attractions

The major attractions in Tarangire National Park include the vegetation zones of which the ***Acacia tortilis*** parkland is the most attractive to visitors. The park is also famous for having many species of birds. The other attraction is the **tree climbing python,** a rare occurrence in other parks.

Well coiled on a trunk of a tree, the python is having a short rest.
But who knows, the next move might be to strike at its enemy.

The undulating **landscape, the Tarangire River, swamps** etc.... add to the fascinating beauty of the park.

The best time to visit the park is between June and November. The park is reached from Arusha by following the Arusha-Dodoma road and then branching off to the left at a place called Kwa-Kuchinja. The gate is about eight kilometres from the main road. The road from Arusha to Kwa-Kuchinja is tarmac; and at a normal touring speed by car, it may take up to two hours to get to Tarangire, 120 kms. away, from Arusha.

Facilities

The Tarangire Safari Camp is a luxury tented camp over-looking the Tarangire River. It has a main building which contains a dining hall, bar, reception office and shop.

The National Park Authority maintains a number of camping sites for people who need a taste of wilderness. Close to the safari camp there is an airstrip for charter planes.

ARUSHA NATIONAL PARK

SUMMARY

Establishment:	1960
Area:	137 Sq. km.
Location:	Situated at latitude 3° 15′ S and longitude 35° 55′ E at its centre.
Principal features:	The rugged Mount Meru, lakes, craters and forest.
Altitude:	Ranges from 1,524m above sea level at Momella to nearly 4,572m at the summit of Meru.
Major attractions:	The Momella lakes, Ngurdoto crater, Meru crater and cone, black and white colobus monkeys, giraffes, forest and water falls.
Best time to visit:	October to February.
Facilities:	Momella Game Lodge; Mount Meru Game Lodge and Tanzanite Hotel at Usa river; Ngaresero Lodge at Tengeru; camping sites; hostel; huts and a garage.

ARUSHA NATIONAL PARK

The Park

THIS is the second smallest park after the Gombe Stream National Park. It has a total area of 137 sq. km. The park, established in 1960, is the only one which has had changed its name three times. Initially, it used to be called the Ngurdoto Crater National Park. By then, the prominent features included the Momella Lakes. When Mount Meru Crater was annexed, the name changed to Meru Crater National Park. Later the name Arusha National Park was adopted.

However, it has been suggested that when the entire natural habitat above the eighteen hundredth contour line is included in the Park, the name should rightly settle as Mount Meru National Park.

The Park, situated at **latitude 3° 15′ S and longitude 35° 55′ E** at its centre is 37 km. away from Arusha. From Arusha the visitor travels for about 21 km. easterly along the tarmac road towards Moshi. And just after the Usa River settlement, there is a turning to the left sign-posted Ngarenanyuki — more correctly, Engarenanyokie in Maasai, meaning brown water — and Arusha National Park. This is an all weather gravel road that climbs by an easy and gentle gradient

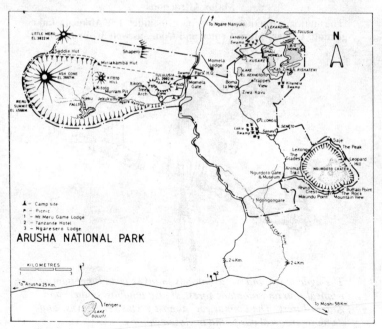

ARUSHA NATIONAL PARK

39

passing through coffee farms on the way to Ngurdoto Gate which is 11 km. from the Moshi road. Within the park, altitudes range from 1524 metres above sea level at Momella to nearly 4572 metres at the summit of Meru.

There are over 50 km. of game viewing road/track in the Ngurdoto and Momella sections of the park. However to protect destruction of the Ngurdoto Crater which is only 3 km. in diameter, no road has been constructed into it. Hence the park's Regulations stipulate that the crater be viewed from several spots established on the rim. The spots include: Buffalo Point, Rock, Mountain view, Mikindani Point, Rhino Crest, Glades, Leitong, Saje, Peak and Leopard Hill. Mount Kilimanjaro can be viewed and photographed conveniently from the Mountain View.

The roads inside the park have been aligned to obtain the best viewing of both animals and scenery. Considering the type of the park, the roads are naturally hilly and twisty. Since they are narrow, it is obvious that big buses should be driven with extra care. A drive through this park is quite enjoyable as there are very romantic scenes; and as is always in a National Park, the slower you go the more you will see.

Major Attractions

The major attractions in this park include: **The Momella Lakes, Ngurdoto Crater, Meru Crater and Cone, as well as the rare Black**

The agile black and white colobus monkey is an inhabitant of tropical rain and montane forest; it also inhabits outliers and gallery forest. The animal eats almost exclusively leaves, and being so arboreal it is found in closed canopy.

and White Colobus monkey. The road up the Meru Crater and Cone, especially above 1829 metres, requires four-wheel-drive vehicles, and even these may get stuck when it is raining. This road rises from 1524 metres to 2439 metres in about 10 km. There are several beauty spots to visit, such as waterfalls before arriving at the base of the cone.

Along this route the scenery and views are superb, for the road passes through virgin forests containing gigantic trees and many open glades where animals are frequently seen. Elephant, buffalo, bushbuck, red **forest duiker** and Colobus monkey being the usual ones observed on the mountain. At the higher levels the wild flowers are lovely. The mountain road ends in the heath zone. From here visitors can walk up the crater.

There are two mountain huts-one is at Miriakamba and the other at the **Saddle**; each of which can accommodate 24 people. Some people may be **disappointed** because there are no lions in this park, but leopards can be spotted. Other animals to be seen are waterbuck, hippo, warthog, bohor reedbuck, did-dik, etc., all of which are of interest. Admittedly, Arusha National Park, once a farm land and popular hunting area, boasts of the **highest density of giraffes** in the world. The Momella Lakes offer the best selection of avifauna. Many northern bird migrants can be seen between May and October.

Giraffes are the tallest of all living land mammals. The animal's typical gait is rather slow, deliberate and remarkably graceful, almost as if the actions were filmed in slow motion.

Facilities

For visitors who just cannot tear themselves away from this miniature paradise, accommodation can be provided at the Momella Game Lodge. This lodge has been built a few metres outside the Park's boundary and close to the Momella Gate. It offers comfortable accommodation in bungalows and thatched rondavels, good food and a spacious lounge with a large open log fire. The Tanzanite Hotel and the Mount Meru Game Lodge are at Usa River settlement; they are within short distance from the park and visitors can use them. The Ngaresero lodge, is slightly further away, at Tengeru.

At the park's Headquarters there is a garage for servicing vehicles, while at Ngurdoto Gate there is a museum for visitor's orientation to the park. For campers, the park has several camping sites where visitors can stay at a much reduced cost. However the park authority does not provide camping equipment and it is the visitors responsibility to bring them along. Some mountain equipment and guides may be hired from the Park Headquarters.

MOUNT KILIMANJARO NATIONAL PARK

SUMMARY

Establishment: 1973

Area: 756 Sq. km.

Location: Situated between latitudes 2° 50' and 3° 10' S and between longitudes 37° 20' and 37° 40' E.

Principal features: Shira plateau, Mawenzi and Kibo peaks.

Altitude: Varies from 1,829m at Marangu gate to 5,895m at Kibo peak.

Major attractions: Kibo peak and rain forest; flowers and the landscape

Best time to visit: September to November.

Facilities: Kibo and Marangu Hotels, hostels, huts, camping sites, porters and guides, mountain equipment.

MOUNTAIN KILIMANJARO NATIONAL PARK

The Park

IT has always been believed that the highest mountain in Africa, a scenic show piece of Tanzania would eventually become a National Park. And indeed it has become one. But one wonders why this was not done earlier. This was probably due to lack of creative urgency. Mountain Kilimanjaro is more or less of a scenic park, rather than a game park.

There are some problems of rare and vanishing animals here, but quite a number of unique and endemic flora. Formerly this area was under the care of the Forestry Division. Funds for initial capital development were provided by the Norwegian Government through NORAD. The funds were used to replace the old huts up the Marangu route; build the headquarters complex at the gate and build a road from the gate down to the junction of the road branching off to Kibo Hotel.

When the project was completed, the park was finally gazetted in 1973 and officially inaugurated in July 1977. To-date the Kilimanjaro

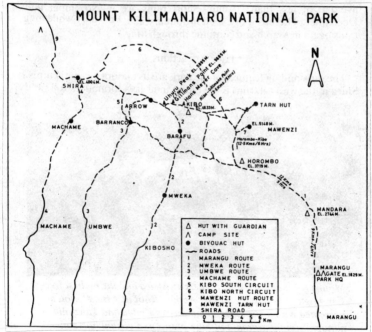

MOUNT KILIMANJARO NATIONAL PARK

Δ HUT WITH GUARDIAN
Λ CAMP SITE
● BIVOUAC HUT
‿ ROADS
1 MARANGU ROUTE
2 MWEKA ROUTE
3 UMBWE ROUTE
4 MACHAME ROUTE
5 KIBO SOUTH CIRCUIT
6 KIBO NORTH CIRCUIT
7 MAWENZI HUT ROUTE
8 MAWENZI TARN HUT
9 SHIRA ROAD

National Park has an area of 756 sq. km. most of which is above the tree line at 2700 metres above sea level. Its complex has an enormous base of about 50 x 80 km. It rises from the dry plains through a wide belt of forest and high alpine zone of heath to an almost bare desert and finally to the snow cap. This park, in northern Tanzania, the home of Chagga people, is only forty eight kilometres from Moshi town or ninety kilometres from the Kilimanjaro International Airport. The park may be reached from the airport in about one and a half hours. The road is bitumenised all the way to the entrance gate.

The people in this area are very industrious and they are famous for their banana and coffee farms, stall feeding of cattle as well as indigenous irrigation. The park headquarters is situated at the Marangu gate at the forest edge. The park is located between **latitudes 2° 50′** and **3° 10′ S** and between **longitudes 37° 20′** and **37° 40′ E**. The **altitude** varies from 1829m at the Marangu gate to 5895m at the snow capped — Kibo peak. Rainfall of 2,337 mm has been recorded in the forest at 1829m elevation. It decreases rapidly with an increase in elevation, with an average of 1321mm at Mandara Hut (2744m). Horombo Hut at 3719m has about 534mm and Kibo Hut 4633m has an average of less than 204mm. Short rains are in November and December. There is a dry spell in January and February while long rains begin in March and continue through May.

Major Attractions

The outstanding features of the park are its major volcanic centres. **Shira** in the west (4004m) is the oldest in its lava formation; followed

Mount Kilimanjaro is the highest in Africa and the highest free-standing outcrop in the world. At the "Roof of Africa", you are presented with a vista that encompasses Kenya and Tanzania — a magnificent panorama of high plains and distant horizons.

by the rugged peak of **Mawenzi** in the east (5148m) while the snow capped **Kibo** (5895m) in the middle is the most recent. The change in vegetation from the surrounding **savannah grassland** to **rain forests, moorland, tundra, semi-desert** and finally to the **"snow of Kilimanjaro"** are other attractions. The forest is a very important genetic storehouse as well as being a water shed for agricultural lands, industrial plants and fishing areas below.

The game animals which can be seen especially in western Kilimanjaro include Harvey's and Abbott's duiker, elephant, buffalo, eland, leopard, colobus and blue monkey.

The duiker is one of the small antelopes found in forests. There are several species varying in size and colour pattern.

Ascent From Marangu

The ascent of Kibo can be made from the **Mweka, Umbwe, Shira, Machame and Rongai.** The most common ascent however, is the **Marangu** route. The YMCA and the State Travel Service Ltd., in Moshi, the Mountain Kilimanjaro National Park, Marangu and Kibo Hotels in Marangu arrange complete trips up to Kibo. They provide guides, porters, lamps and all food and utensils as well as booking the huts.

Climbing Mountain Kilimanjaro takes five days-three days ascent and two days descent. This mountain may be climbed anytime of the year, but from March to May, there are long rains. During this period the route is slippery and this makes it uncomfortable for climbers. Climbers begin their "ant like labour" at the Marangu gate. They walk through the rain forest to Mandara Hut for about three to four hours. It is approximately **9 kilometres** from the gate.

The first night is spent in this hut. Surrounding the hut is some very attractive forest scenery. Close by there is the **Maundi Crater** which can be visited after a short rest. The next day, a short, steep walk is made out of the forest into the moorland. As one approaches Horombo Hut the land becomes very rocky. The distance between the two huts is **12 kilometres** and is reached after about five hours. Horombo Hut is situated at a very scenic point.

On the left just over the ridge, stands the Kibo Peak, shimmering in the sun; and on the right stands the rocky, majestic Mawenzi, towering over the hut. After a night's rest one continues past the cactus like giant groundsel and the "last water point". The path leads up between the two main peaks — Mawenzi and Kibo. At this point the average climber will begin to feel the effects of the altitude cautioning one to tread slowly and just enjoy the flora and the scenery. But the remedy for this is to walk slowly and rest for few minutes after every half an hour's walk.

When at last the "saddle" is reached, the climber will find himself walking across a miniature desert. For several kilometres around there is nothing but barren rock and sand. Gradually the path steepens, and Kibo Hut is reached. The distance between Horombo Hut and Kibo Hut is **12½ kilometres.** It takes about five to six hours between the points. The trial begins about past midnight the following morning. As warmly clothed as possible the climber begins the slow tiring trudge up the scree, resting after every few hundred metres.

Only one thing breaks the monotony of the climb and that is the sunrise behind the Mawenzi Peak — a sight that will never be forgotten. Hans Meyer Cave is passed half way up the scree slope, but after this landmark, the slope steepens and the last few hundred feet below Gillman's point never seem to end. This point is **3½ km.** from Kibo Hut and takes about 5 hours.

It is obvious that on reaching Gillman's point one needs a rest. When one has revived, the crater is traversed clockwise to Uhuru peak which is reached in about forty-five minutes from Gillman's point. Uhuru peak is the highest point in Africa. The piles of snow at the peak and the crater, the undulating landscape below and the overall scenery of the mountain is very fascinating. Hemingway apathy describes the scenery of the mountain in his famous book — Snows of Kilimanjaro — thus, **"as wide as all the world, great, high, and unbelievable white in the sun, was the square top of Kilimanjaro".**

Descending is easier and the fourth night is spent at Horombo Hut; while on the fifth day, one gets to Marangu gate. Hang gliding has also been tried but for further information contact the park authorities.

Facilities

Visitors to this park can be accommodated at the YMCA Hostel or Moshi Hotel in Moshi; Marangu and Kibo Hotels in Marangu. There are also two hostels at the Kilimanjaro National Park's Headquarters. With the exception of Moshi Hotel, the rest arrange complete trips up the mountain. It is of necessity that climbers are suitably clothed and equipped. Hence warm clothing, dark glasses, boots, Balaclava helment, mittens, sleeping bags, a first aid kit, and so forth, are all necessary for climbers. These are provided by the respective hotels. In addition to equipment, the hotels provide guides, porters, food, utensils, etc.

Along the Marangu route, there are three huts where climbers spend their nights: Mandara Hut has several units which can accommodate sixty people; Horombo, the second hut, is the largest of all stations. It is a meeting point for ascending and descending people, with a capacity of 120 people. Kibo Hut takes sixty people too. In these huts there are bunks with mattresses and water is available in each station. There is radio communication at Horombo and Kibo Huts. These stations can communicate directly with the Headquarters at the gate whenever necessary.

There is also a well trained Rescue Team for those who fall sick due to effects of high altitude. They have stretchers and first-aid kits for these victims. A garage and a dispensary are at the Park Headquarters.

MIKUMI NATIONAL PARK

SUMMARY

Establishment:	**1964**
Area:	**3,230 Sq. km.**
Location:	**Situated between latitudes 7° 00' and 7° 50' S and between longitudes 37° 00' and 37° 30' E.**
Principal features:	**Mkata river flood plain, Swamps and the miombo woodlands.**
Altitude:	**549m above sea level.**
Major attractions:	**The Mkata river flood plains, herds of buffaloes and elephants and the black and white colobus monkeys in the south.**
Best time to visit:	**September to December.**
Facilities:	**Mikumi Wildlife Lodge, Mikumi Wildlife Tented Camp, Camping sites, Youth hostel, garage, petrol station and an airstrip.**

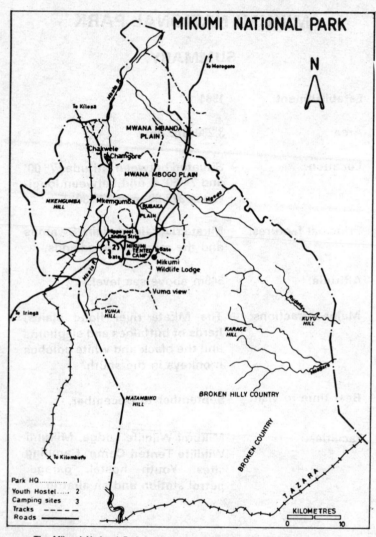

MIKUMI NATIONAL PARK

N

To Morogoro

To Kilosa

MWANA MBANDA
PLAIN

Chakwele
Chamgore

MWANA MBOGO PLAIN

MKEMGUMBA
HILL

Mkemgumba

RUBAKA
PLAIN

Hippo pool
Landing Strip

MIKUMI
TENTED
CAMP

Gate

Gate

Gate

Mikumi
Wildlife Lodge

Vuma view

To Iringa

VUMA
HILL

KARAGE
HILL

KUYU
HILL

NATAMBIKO
HILL

BROKEN HILLY COUNTRY

BROKEN COUNTRY

To Kilombero

T A Z A R A

Park HQ	1
Youth Hostel	2
Camping sites	3
Tracks	-----
Roads	

KILOMETRES

0   10

*The Mikumi National Park borders with the Selous Wildlife Reserve in the
South. The Tanzania-Zambia Railway line which marks the boundary is an important infrastructure for the "Southern tourist circuit."*

MIKUMI NATIONAL PARK

The Park

MIKUMI National Park is in Morogoro Region, in the southern tourist circuit of Tanzania. This is the nearest park to the commercial capital of Tanzania, Dar es Salaam. It is about 288 km. west of the city and takes about four hours by car to get there. The road is bitumenised all the way through to the Park. The Park gazetted in 1964 gets its name from the settlement of Mikumi which in turn, gets its name from the spindle-shaped borassus palm trees which are typical of the area. Mikumi National Park with an area of 3230 sq. km is the fifth largest park. The park is located between **latitudes 7° 00′** and **7° 50′ S** and between **longitudes 37° 00′** and **37° 30′ E.** It lies between the villages of Doma and Mikumi on the Dar es Salaam-Tunduma road. The Park Headquarters lies at an elevation of 549 m above sea level.

The principal features of Mikumi are the Mkata River-flood plain, with its hardpan, ridges, swamps and black-clay grassland, the miombo woodlands on the hill to the east and west, and the rivers with their fringe of tall trees and dense thickets. Rainfall varies throughout the park in different zones. At the Park Headquarters for instance, the average rainfall is 508 mm per annum, while at Chamgore, 24 km away is 635 mm. In the hills it is as high as 1067 mm. The short rains usually fall during November and December. Long rains are from March to May.

Major Attractions

The park contains a spectacular concentration and variety of wildlife. **The Mkata River flood plains** form a horse-shoe of hills, and are the feeding grounds of large herds of buffalo and wandering groups of elephant. The wooded fringes of the plains harbour many wildebeest, zebra, impala, baboon, warthog, jackal, etc. particularly during the heat of the day.

The best time to visit the park is from June through February.

Facilities

There is one lodge and one tented camp in Mikumi. The Mikumi Wildlife Lodge which is managed by the Tanzania Tourist Corporation is built on a spur over looking a valley at an altitude of 762m. There are 50 self-contained double bedrooms. There is also a swimming pool and the Park authority runs a petrol station and an office at this lodge. In case of trouble with your car, you may service it at the garage which is just behind the Park Headquarters.

Two adult male buffaloes clash in single combat. These ferocious fights, spectacular but rarely fatal, may have a female or a piece of territory at stake but also serve as outlets for aggressive feelings and release of nervous tension.

A gift shop is housed in the lodge. Close to the gate there is a tented camp over looking an expanse of plain and low valley in which game is usually seen. This is the Mikumi Wildlife Tented Camp. It is managed by the Oyster Bay Hotel, Dar es Salaam to whom bookings should be made. The camp has more than ten tents. There is a Youth Hostel at the Park Headquarters with a capacity of 48 people. Like all other Youth Hostels in th Parks, visitors should book direct to the Warden In-Charge and should also bring all beddings.

Camping sites are maintained and the would-be campers are required to pay the fees before they are shown where to camp. It is also possible to fly in from Dar es Salaam or Arusha as there is an airstrip near the Park Headquarters which is serviceable to light aircraft throughout the year.

RUAHA NATIONAL PARK

SUMMARY

Establishment:	1964
Area:	12,950 Sq. km.
Location:	Situated at latitude 7° 45′ S and longitude 35° 40′ E at its centre.
Principal features:	Rivers, escarpment, springs, hills, miombo woodland.
Altitude:	750 to 1,900m above sea level.
Major attractions:	Great Ruaha river, elephants, kudus, hippos and crocodiles.
Best time to visit:	July to December.
Facilities:	Msembe camp, Ruaha River Camp, camping sites, garage and an airstrip.

RUAHA NATIONAL PARK

The Park

RUAHA is 12,950 sq. km. in area, the third largest park in Tanzania. It is situated at **latitude 7° 45′ S** and **longitude 35° 40 E** at its centre. The park, previously part of the Rungwa Game Reserve, was detached from the reserve and declared a national park in 1964. This big chunk of land gets its name from the Great Ruaha River which flows along the entire eastern border of the park for about 160 km.

It is from this river that most of Tanzania gets its electricity. The power is generated at Kidatu on the river. The capital city of Dodoma also gets its power from the same river, further upstream, at Mtera. The river joins the Ulanga, to make the Rufiji River, many kilometres downstream. The river changes in character over this stretch. There are rocky rapids alternating with deep pools and in some places, it becomes a shallow river of many channels wandering between numerous sandbanks.

The name Ruaha, which has been borrowed from the river and applied to the park as a whole, is a corruption of **Luvaha** which simply means "great" in the Hehe language.

A good all weather road now connects the Park Headquarters with Iringa via Mloa by passing through Idodi. The Ruaha River is crossed by a ferry, within the park, at **Ibuguziwa.** Plans are underway to build a bridge at Ibuguziwa. Although the distance can be covered in less time, it is best to allow four hours from Iringa to reach the park in comfort.

The park headquarters at Msembe is 112 km. from Iringa; 615 km. from Dar es Salaam; 322 km. from Mikumi; 369 km from Dodoma; 502 km. from Mbeya and 807 km. from Arusha. It is exactly half way from the Tanzania-Zambia border town of Tunduma to Dar es Salaam; and a visit to the park is a perfect reason for breaking an otherwise tiring journey. The best months for visiting the park are July to November. The grass is long from February to June, thus restricting game viewing. January, February and March are wet months and many tracks become impassable while animal density especially along the rivers, thins out.

The elevation of the park varies from 750 metres in the Great Ruaha Valley to 1,700 metres at the summit of Datambulwa mountain in the south and 1,900 metres on Ikingu mountain in the west.

The rainfall varies from an average of 520 mm. per annum at Msembe, the Park Headquarters, to more than 800mm. per annum above the escarpment in the Miombo country. It falls during the months of December, January, February, March and April.

57

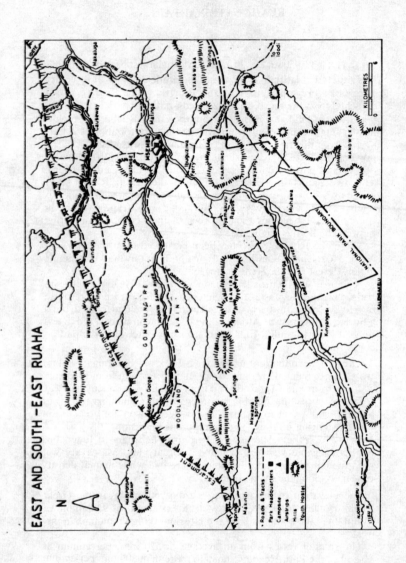

EAST AND SOUTH-EAST RUAHA

There are several ecological zones in the Ruaha National Park. The four main ones are: The main river valleys with their stands of tall fig trees; areas of open "black cotton" grassland; the Miombo or *Brachystegia* woodlands and the undulating country which is dominated by the baobab trees but which mainly consists of species of *Combretum* and *Commiphora* trees and shrubs. Within these habitats are different animal species in order of tolerance and preference. As is always the case, these zones are a lifebelt to wild animals.

Major Attractions

Ruaha National Park enjoys, a good climate and indeed it is, a photographer's paradise. Without any exaggeration, this area contains a vast tract of completely unspoiled Africa, and is one of Tanzania's largest **elephant** sanctuaries.

An elephant is the largest terrestrial mammal. Males weigh up to six tons and females about four tons. This mixed feeder requires an average of 300 kg. of food a day. Its gestation period is about 22 months and the life span is approximately 60 years.

The exciting **Great Ruaha River** offers the major attraction, of course, especially during the dry season. In this period the river attracts a large number of impala, warthog, giraffe, waterbuck, eland, zebra, buffalo, lion, leopard, hunting dog, Grant's gazelle, roan and sable antelopes, cheetah, etc... in an almost endless list. Nowhere in East Africa can you see such a big concentration of Lesser and Great kudu as in this park. Admittedly, the river harbours an unbelievable high number of **hippo schools** and **crocodile** which merit attention.

The kudus are some of the most handsome antelopes in the parks. In Tanzania they are commonly found in Ruaha.

Facilities

There are modern hotels in Iringa town where visitors can stay in transit to or from Ruaha National Park. They include the Isimila Hotel, which is close to the Railway Bus Station; Sunset Motel along the Dar es Salaam-Mbeya road; Railway Hotel and Ruaha International Guest House. However, a new hotel in the park — Ruaha River Camp, has been opened 10 km. south of Msembe. Perched on a rock, this structure, provides comfortable accommodation and good food.

It blends perfectly well with its surroundings and its position commands spectacular views. Provided prior arrangements are made, visitors can have excursion tours organized by the camp; and those arriving with their own transport, can buy fuel from here, depending on its availability.

At the Park Headquarters, Msembe, there is a permanent camp. It consists of rondavels each with beds. Most of the essential equipment are provided, except food and drinks which visitors must bring with them. Camping is also permitted on areas set aside by the park authority. Apart from the ferry at Ibuguziwa, there is also an airstrip near the Headquarters, catering for charter planes, so that the park is accessible not only by road but also by air.

There is a garage at Msembe, but supplies are quite unreliable.

Although it may be helpful to service vehicles here, visitors are advised to bring with them all the essential vehicle accessories, and enough gasoline, for their safari back to Iringa.

NOTES ———————————————

KATAVI NATIONAL PARK

SUMMARY

Establishment: 1974

Area: 2,253 Sq. km

Location: Situated between latitudes 6° 40' and 7° 05' S and between longitudes 30° 50'and 31° 30' E.

Principal features: Lakes, rivers, swamps and miombo woodland.

Altitude: 900m above sea level.

Major attractions: Lakes Katavi and Chada connected by Katuma river, miombo woodland and plains.

Best time to visit: July to October.

Facilities: Hotels, lodges and petrol stations in Mpanda town; camping sites in the park.

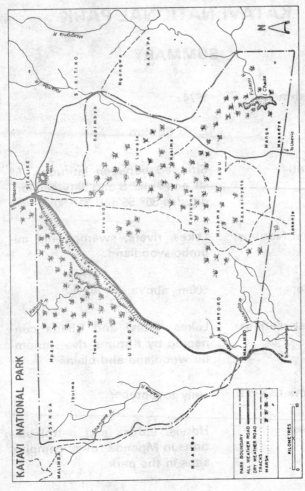

The Katavi National Park forms part of the "Western tourist circuit" along with Mahale and Gombe Stream. This park has very romantic scenes that may baffle all description: Lakes Katavi and Chada connected by Katuma river are memorable sites.

KATAVI NATIONAL PARK

The Park

IT WAS the people of Mpanda in the Rukwa Region of Tanzania who initiated the Government to raise the status of this area to that of a national park, so as to ensure that this piece of land would remain a national heritage for their children to enjoy. For Tanzania National Parks, this is the best possible indication of the success the authority has managed to achieve in seeking greater public understanding of the people's role in the parks. Indeed this is an encouragement to all people who value conservation, not only in Tanzania but the world over. Funds for initial development were donated by the Frankfurt Zoological Society, West Germany.

The work there has so far included the marking out of the boundary of the park, putting in some tracks and keeping up anti-poaching patrols. The Katavi National Park, with an area of 2253 sq. km, was gazetted in 1974. It is situated some 40 km. southeast of Mpanda town astride the main Mpanda Sumbawanga road.

Geographically it is located between **latitudes 6° 40′** and **7° 05′ S** and between **longitudes 30° 50′** and **31° 30′ E.** The altitude in the park is about 900 metres above sea level. In this park, like in most other parks, in the country, long rains begin in March and continues to May.

The main type of vegetation found in this area is the **miombo** woodland. The forest is interspersed with *Acacia* particularly in the vicinity of Lake Chada. There are also open and short-grassed flood plains.

Major Attractions

The main features of attractions in the park include **Lake Katavi** with its vast, short grassed flood plains in the north; palm fringed **Lake Chada** (some 64 sq. km.) in the south-east and the **Katuma River** which connects these two lakes. The river is more of a vast swamp than a river. The park is mainly flat or undulating with low hills in the northern section of the area.

The flood plains are covered with black cotton soil but the rest of the park consists of sandy soils. The noteworthy fauna include: elephant, buffalo, zebra, topi, hippo, sable and roan antelopes; also eland, leopard, lion and crocodile. Apart from mammals and reptiles, there are many species of waterfowls.

Hippos and crocodiles spend most of the day in the water, being able to swim completely submerged and to walk or rest on the river bed.

Facilities

There are hotels and lodges at Mpanda and Sumbawanga towns for visitors travelling to Katavi National Park. While in the park, visitors may use camping sites set up by the park authority. It is essential therefore, for campers to carry with them camping equipment, food cooking and eating utensils. It is also important for visitors to come with enough petrol which can take them back to either Mpanda or Sumbawanga.

Unfortunately this park does not have all the essential facilities required by visitors. It is therefore a park for those people who can face this challenge. No doubt, as visitors to the park increase, and the park income improves, so visitor facilities will get better.

MAHALE MOUNTAINS NATIONAL PARK

SUMMARY

Establishment: 1985

Area: 1,577 Sq. km.

Location: Situated between latitudes 6° 00' and 6° 28' S and between longitudes 29° 43' and 30° 07' E.

Principal features: Lake, mountain range, rift valley and forests.

Altitude: 2,000 to 2,462m above sea level.

Major attractions: Chimpanzees, Lake Tanganyika, waterfalls, birds, mountains and forests.

Best time to visit: May to October.

Facilities: Camping sites, porters and guides, guest house and boats.

MAHALE MOUNTAINS NATIONAL PARK

The Park

THIS park is situated slightly over 150km. south of Kigoma, and it can be located between **latitudes 6° 00′** and **6° 28′ S and between longitudes 29° 43′** and **30° 07 E.** Since at present there is no overland access to this area except for a track from Lagosa via Mwese to Mpanda town, it can be reached by a laborious 10-16 hour journey in a small vessel from Kigoma. However from Kigoma, visitors may catch a scheduled steamer, *Mv Liemba* or *Mwongozo* to Lagosa (Mugambo) which takes close to 6 hours. The ship stops in the bay for loading and unloading, so visitors must get on one of the private boats going to the shore. From here, another 3 hours by boat, takes you to Kasoge, in Mahale. When services develop, it is proposed to operate a regular ferry boat so as to link the park with Tanzania's western tourist circuit, around Lake Tanganyika, to which it belongs along with Gombe and Katavi.

Mahale has two seasons: Dry season and rainy season. But, due to variations observed over the years, it has been difficult to draw with precision the border line between the two seasons. However, the dry season begins at the end of May and continues through October. During this period the lake is normally calm at night.

Admittedly, the rainy season which is normally longer than the dry season is from October to January, and then March to May. At night, both in the dry and rainy seasons it becomes quite cool, the minimum temperature being around 15° C in July and August. Annual rainfall ranges from 1500 and 2500mm.

The length of the park is about 50 km. It has a total area of 1577 sq.km. Its western boundary is the shore of Lake Tanganyika. The Mahale Mountains range at the middle part of the east side of Lake Tanganyika, forms a part of the eastern wall of the western Rift Valley. The topographical features of the Mahale area represent a cross section of the history of the earth.

The National Park runs North North West to South South East with an elevation range of 2,000 to 2,400m. In the Western part of Tanzania, it is one of the longest mountain ranges. Its highest peak, Mount Nkungwe, has an elevation of 2,462 metres above sea level.

Major Attractions

There are numerous species of animals in the park. The common ones include the blue duiker, sharpe's grysbok, bushy-tailed mongoose, banded mongoose, red legged sun-squirrel, brush-tailed porcupines, red colobus monkey, Angolan black-and-white colobus monkey. The Angolan black-and-white colobus monkey of Mount

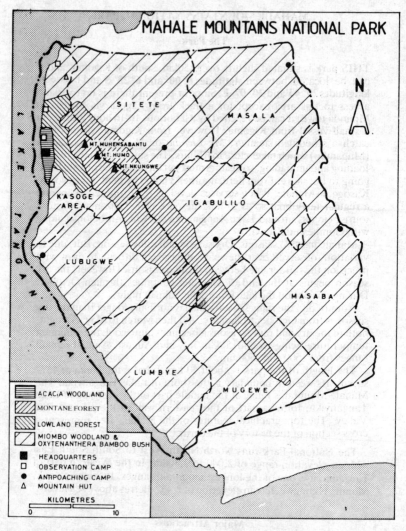

MAHALE MOUNTAINS NATIONAL PARK

SITETE

MASALA

MT MUHENSABANTU
MT. HUMO
MT. NKUNGWE

KASOGE
AREA

IGABULILO

LUBUGWE

MASABA

LUMBYE

MUGEWE

ACACIA WOODLAND
MONTANE FOREST
LOWLAND FOREST
MIOMBO WOODLAND &
OXYTENANTHERA BAMBOO BUSH
HEADQUARTERS
OBSERVATION CAMP
ANTIPOACHING CAMP
MOUNTAIN HUT
KILOMETRES
0   10

Nkungwe is very likely here-to-fore unknown and distinct subspecies. Some animals such as leopard, buffalo and lion, which were never or rarely seen before have appeared on the scene.

The most remarkable creature of the park, however, is the **chimpanzee.** It is estimated that there are about 1,000 chimpanzees which can be seen in groups of 5s up to 30s in their natural habitat. Scientists, mostly from Japan, have been studying these animals for over 20 years. More than 100 chimpanzees have been habituated and named individually. Apart from the famous chimpanzee, Mahale can offer **mountain climbing.** Although mountain climbing has not yet been developed, the Mahale mountain range is quite ideal in this sport. The mountain range has six prominent peaks with the highest being Mount Nkungwe. Other peaks which stand beyond 2,000m. are: Humo, Muhensabantu and Pasagalu to the north of Mount Nkungwe and Sibindi, Mfitwa, Sisanga and Tambila to the south of it.

The mountains are heavily ravined with numerous valleys and streams that intersect the mountains. Some of the valleys support permanent streams that flow into Lake Tanganyika. Some **waterfalls** can also be sighted in certain areas of the park. Open woodland areas between the mountain ranges, can be observed. Mahale also offers wonderful opportunities for **bird watchers.** The birds include: Livingstone's touraco, crested guinea fowl, crowned hawk-eagle, ducks and geese, sandpiper, giant king fisher; the others are African fish eagle, paradise fly catcher and trumpeter hornbill. There is no doubt, bird lovers visiting the Mahale would increasingly find pleasure in the spectacular diverse in bird life.

Ornithologists find Tanzania a good place for studying birds. There are so many bird species that some have remained unidentified in certain localities.

The other attraction is **Lake Tanganyika.** This is the longest lake in the world (720km) and the second deepest (1435m) after Lake Baykal (1740m) in Russia. The bottom of Lake Tanganyika is 655m. below sea level. This park is unique in **botanogeographical terms** in that it is the meeting place of natural scenic grandeur of Lake Tanganyika, Mahale Mountain range, Zairen tropical rain forests and Tabora Miombo woodlands. It is the only park in Tanzania affording the opportunity to observe together a wide variety of wildlife with home-lands in eastern, western and southern Africa.

Of all the areas along Lake Tanganyika, the Mahale areas is one of the richest in topographical variation, and its imposing mountain chain makes for splendid scenic harmony with the lake. A beautiful view of the lake can be observed from the main ridge of the Mahale chain. This **"foot-walking national park"** was opened in July 1984 but was officially gazetted on 14th June, 1985.

Facilities

The quickest way to reach Mahale is by air. This can be done through Air Tanzania from Dar es Salaam to Kigoma. The other way is to go through Nairobi to Bujumbura and Kigoma and finally to Mahale by steamship. There are plans to build an airstrip at Sitolo — the proposed Park Headquarters, for charter planes. Kigoma can also be reached from Dar es Salaam via Tabora by train. Although the journey takes about 40 hours to cover, it is nonetheless a rewarding experience. Throughout the journey, the countryside changes in character from time to time. At the end of it all, one would have built an impression that one was probably riding in a different world.

Swimming and scuba diving is possible and visitors are advised to bring along their own equipment. And for those who would like to attempt to climb the Mahale Mountains range, the suggested list of equipment to take along would include boots, fairly warm clothings, light tents, sleeping bags, torches and caned food. Guides and porters may be provided by the centre. The ascent to the highest peak and descent may take three days.

Visitors with camping equipment are allowed to camp in the park in camping sites. It is important for visitors to have enough food to last the whole safari as supplies are not yet reliable. Although there is a guest house, it is practical to be equipped with cooking and eating utensils, stoves, bed-sheets, toilet paper rolls and other essentials. In transit to Mahale, visitors can be accommodated at the Kigoma Railways Hotel.

GOMBE STREAM NATIONAL PARK

SUMMARY

Establishment: 1968

Area: 52 Sq. km.

Location: Situated between latitude 4° 40′ S and longitude 29° 38′ E at its centre.

Principal features: Mountains, lake, rift valley.

Altitude: 681 to 1,524m. above sea level.

Major attractions: Chimpanzees, Lake Tanganyika, valleys with streams, Kakombe water fall.

Best time to visit: Throughout the year.

Facilities: Hostel, camping sites, guides and boats.

GOMBE STREAM NATIONAL PARK

The Park

ABOUT 16 km. north of Kigoma in the north-western part of Tanzania, lies the Gombe Stream National Park. This is the smallest park in Tanzania. It is only 52 sq.km. in area and was established in

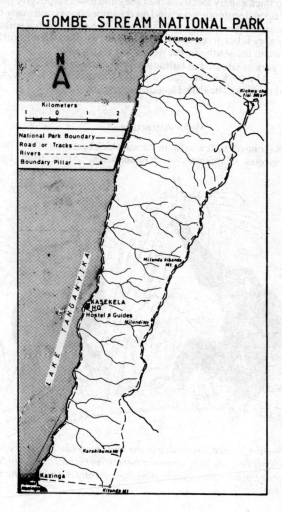

1968. The Gombe Stream National Park consists of a narrow mountainous strip of country stretching for some 16 km. along the eastern shore of Lake Tanganyika and running inland about 5 km. to the peaks of the mountain range forming the Rift escarpment. These mountains rise steeply from the Lake (681m) to heights of about 1524m. Many steepsided valleys and ravines intersect the mountains, a number of which support permanent streams.

The thick gallery forests of the valley and lower slopes give place to more open deciduous woodland on the upper slopes and many of the peaks and ridges are covered with grass. The park which is within the Rift Valley is bordered by two villages: Mwamgongo in the north and Kazinga in the south. To the west is Lake Tanganyika.

This park is situated at **latitude 4° 40'S** and **longitude 29°38 E** at its centre. The park offers guided tours, and an escort is provided by armed rangers. The Park Headquarters is at Kasekela.

Major Attraction

This is one of the few areas in Africa which harbours one of the most rare species of animals — **Chimpanzees.** Apart from Mahale

The chimpanzee is regarded as the most man-like of all the apes, not only because of its anatomy but also in respect of certain features of behaviour ranging from community defence to the use of tools.

Mountains south of Kigoma, there is nowhere else in Tanzania where chimpanzees can be observed in the wild. Chimpanzees are very amusing and intelligent animals and it is very interesting to observe them in their natural habitats engaged in different activities. The other primates found in the park are: baboon, red colobus monkey, and blue monkey. Bushbuck, buffalo, and leopard are also present in the park.

The other most picturesque feature is the **Kakombe riverine** waterfall which is near the Chimpanzee Research Station. Kigoma is also a historical town. Thus, apart from visiting the park, one may wish to visit other places of interest such as the historical place where Dr. David Livingstone and Stanley met at Ujiji. It was here where Stanley left an imprint with his famous words when he said: **'Dr. Livingstone, I presume'**, when they met at Ujiji on 10 November 1871.

Facilities

There is a hostel for 15 people in the park. Beds, mattresses, and utensils are provided at the hostel. But visitors are required to bring their own food which can be easily obtained at Kigoma. Camping in the park is allowed on special request. Visitors may be accommodated at the Railway Hotel, Lake View Hotel, or Community Centre in Kigoma while in transit to Gombe.

Air Tanzania has regular flights to Kigoma; and there is also a train service several times a week. Unfortunately exact departure days do vary occasionally. The train journey takes about two days from D'Salaam but it is rewarding indeed. From Kigoma, visitors are ferried by boat to Gombe.

RUBONDO ISLAND NATIONAL PARK

SUMMARY

Establishment: 1977

Area: 240 Sq. km.

Location: Situated at latitude 2° 30' S and longitude 31° 45' E at its centre.

Principal features: Lake; about a dozen small islets which belong to the park; forest.

Altitude: 1,150m above sea level.

Major attractions: Sitatunga, birds and the beach. Lake Victoria is another attraction.

Best time to visit: November to February.

Facilities: Huts, camping sites, boats, lorry, guides and an airstrip.

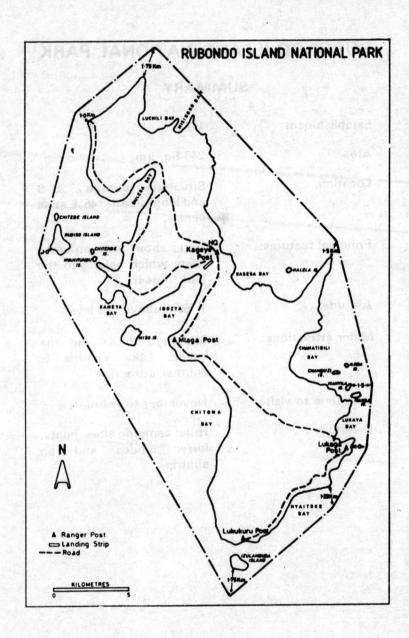

RUBONDO ISLAND NATIONAL PARK

A Ranger Post
Landing Strip
- - - Road

KILOMETRES
0   5

RUBONDO ISLAND NATIONAL PARK

The Park

RUBONDO National Park, was gazetted in 1977. The park is situated north-west of Mwanza at **latitude 2° 30′ S** and **longitude 31° 45′ E** at its centre. It has an area of 240 sq.km and is surrounded by about a dozen smaller islets which belong to the park.

Rubondo National Park has several vegetation types ranging from savannah and open woodland to dense forest and papyrus swamps. The park has many seasonal streams and only a few are permanent. The water table of the island is quite high. In view of this the forests are dense and evergreen. The National Park may be reached from Mwanza in six to seven hours by car via Sengerema-Geita — Nzera and Nkome. From Nkome one takes a boat and the park is reached in two hours. It is about 300 km from Mwanza by this route.

The other alternative is to take a car or bus from Mwanza and drive via Sengerema-Geita-Chato-Mnganza and from there in thirty minutes by boat. When this route is used, the journey may take about ten hours. Unlike other parks, the park authority has prohibited bringing cars on the island. Hence there are guided tours led by park rangers who are usually armed. There are no large predators in the park and so there is no danger of being devoured. Apart from guided tours, there are boat trips to different spots on the area surrounding it.

Major Attractions

The major attraction on Rubondo Island National Park is the presence of many **sitatunga**. This species of animal is indigenous on the island and cannot be found in any other park in Tanzania (except Selous).

As one walks on the island it is a normal sight to bypass a bushbuck hardly five metres away. Some animals are so tame that it is hard to believe that they are wild. One other major attraction is that animals having combined features of a **bushbuck** and a **sitatunga** may be sighted. It is probably true then that the two animals interbreed. Further scientific analysis is required to prove these findings.

The other indigenous species of animals are: hippo, crocodile, vervet monkey, marsh mongoose, genet, pythons which can swallow animals the size of a bush buck. Others include: snakes of different species — poisonous and non poisonous. Among them are green mamba, cobra, viper and other tree snakes. There are also a variety of butterflies. Several other animals which have been transplanted on to the island include: giraffe, elephant, rhino, black and white colobus monkey and chimpanzee.

Sitatungas prefer swamps and marshes. When they walk, the 15-18 cm long hooves expand the moment they come into contact with the ground. The animals are also good swimmers.

This place has also different species of birds, including migrants from Europe and South Africa. Among others, the birds include: fish eagle, martial eagle, goliath heron, sacred ibis, several species of kingfishers, cuckoos, bee eaters etc. It is an ideal place for **bird watching.** There is a **good beach** for visitors.

Facilities

There are camping sites on the island. However, visitors should bring all necessary camping equipment as the park does not provide adequate camping or hostel facilities. Cooking and eating utensils, toilet paper, food and matches should not be forgotten. But the park authority has built two *bandas* (huts) which contains three beds each. For these two bandas, bed sheets, blankets, lamps and cooking utensils are available. Nevertheless, food, matches and toilet paper rolls have to be brought from the mainland by the people intending to use these huts.

There is also an air strip at the Park Headquarters, Kageye — which is about one kilometre long and is capable of handling light aircrafts such as *Cessna and Supercub.* There are three boats one of which is capable of carrying twenty people. They are used for travelling on the lake and visiting other small islands which are close by. The boats are hired per hour. The park can be contacted by radio call at No. 5011. The park authority normally switches on the radio at 10.00 hours and closes at 11.00 hours.

A Unimog lorry is also present and can be hired by visitors to take them around the park.

NOTES

UZUNGWA MOUNTAINS NATIONAL PARK

SUMMARY

Establishment: Proposed

Area: About 1,000 Sq. km.

Location: Situated at latitude 7° 45′ S and longitude 36° 36′ E at its centre.

Principal features: Forest reserves.

Altitude: Ranges from 300m. to 2,800m. above sea level.

Major attractions: Primates notably the Iringa red colobus monkey, Sanje mangabey, Sykes monkeys and black and white colobus monkey, birds and the forest.

Best time to visit: September to December.

Facilities: Not available but may use the ones available at Mikumi National Park as well as lodges and guest houses at Kidatu and Ifakara towns.

UZUNGWA MOUNTAINS NATIONAL PARK

The Park

THE Uzungwa is situated at **latitude 7° 45′ S** and **longitude 36° 36′ E**
at its centre. It is connected   by an all weather murram road from
Kidatu to Ifakara; and since it is only ten kilometres south of Mikumi
National Park, during its infancy stage it can certainly be
administered from Mikumi. The park will have a total area of
approximately 1000 sq.km. covering two districts, namely Kilombero
district (Mwanihana Forest Reserve) in Morogoro region and Iringa
district (West Kilombero Scarp Forest Reserve) in Iringa region.

The area spans a great altitudinal range in East Africa ranging from
300m. to 2800m. Admittedly, this range gives greater forest
community diversity, and in some areas rainfall is as high as 3000mm.
per annum. Strictly speaking, the Uzungwa Forests form an
important genetic plant pool in that many of the plants which have
been identified todate cannot be found elsewhere the world over. It is
very likely then that many other plant species remain unidentified.
Some of the plants found in the park include the following:— *Albizia
adiantifolia, Chlorophora excelsa, Macaranga -capense,
Cephalospheara usambarensis, Nuxia congesta, Phoenix reclinata,
Celtis africana and Podocarpus latifolius.* From the botanical research
point of view therefore, this place is an ideal natural laboratory.

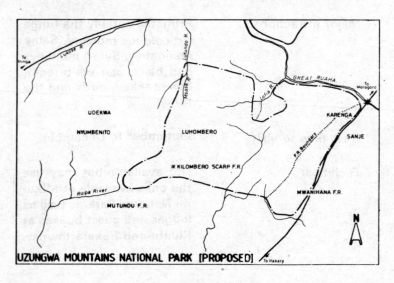

UZUNGWA MOUNTAINS NATIONAL PARK [PROPOSED]

Major Attractions

Apart from the forest which acts as a watershed and having a large number of endemic species both of animals and plants, the park has spectacular mountains scenery, grasslands, rocks, rivers and waterfalls. As it is with other parks, Uzungwa supports a large number of large mammals. The animals include elephant, buffalo, lion, leopard, sable, eland, waterbuck, duiker and bushbuck. But over and above perhaps the most spectacular sight is the presence of two endemic species of primates. These are: the **Iringa red colobus monkey** and the **Sanje mangabey.** The other primates are vervet monkey, baboon, Sykes monkey, black and white colobus monkey.

The red colobus monkey is in danger of being exterminated by man. However the government is doing all it can to ensure that the next generation may also see this beautiful primate.

On the other hand, the Uzungwa is also a paradise in avifauna. It is with no doubt that the area is the richest forest bird locality in Tanzania. The birds found here include sunbird, bush shrike, white-starred forest robin, and hundreds of other species which cannot be named here.

Facilities

At the moment there are no facilities that have been developed as yet. But due to its proximity to Mikumi National Park, the would be visitors shall certainly enjoy all facilities available at Mikumi. The facilities include camping sites, lodges, a youth hostel, a petrol station and a garage at the park's headquarters. At Kidatu and Ifakara, visitors to the park will be able to get simple lodge and food.

As soon as the park is opened, the Tanzania National Parks Authority has plans to establish camping sites. But visitors are warned that the park authority does not provide camping equipment. It is up to the clients therefore to ensure that they carry all the necessary equipment including food.

With the establishment of this area as a national park, the southern tourist circuit would certainly be widened. Hence from the beach in Dar es Salaam a tourist may then go to Selous Wildlife Reserve, come down to Mikumi and Uzungwa and finish off with the spice island — Zanzibar and Mafia island — the conchologist's paradise.

MARINE PROTECTED AREAS IN TANZANIA.

There are many potential marine areas in Tanzania. But since independence, emphasis has been on terrestrial national parks only; no single marine park has been established. Before it is too late, these areas have to be defended from all forms of human interference.

MARINE PARKS FOR TANZANIA

TANZANIA has a distinguished record of achievement in terrestrial conservation. As we go to press, it has thirteen national parks (including Ngorongoro Conservation Area and Selous) and many wildlife reserves. Yet, it is true that marine species have been little studied and there is little biological data to base their conservation.

This is probably due to insufficient trained personnel capable of planning and implementing marine and coastal conservation programmes; no defined national policy with which to deal with marine conservation; lack of financial resources for the development of marine conservation, etc.

It is unquestionably obvious that estuaries, mangrove forests, coral reefs, seagrass beds, submarine banks as well as rocky reefs are all important habitats for fisheries and they call for proper conservation management.

Tanzania has several areas which, if well protected and developed, can be very potential "Marine National Parks". These areas include: Tanga Coral Gardens, Dar es Salaam Coral Gardens, Latham Island Reserve, Mafia Island — Rufiji Delta Reserve and Kilwa Reserve. These areas lie between **latitudes 5° 00′** and **9° 00′ S** and between **longitudes 39° 00′** and **40° 00′ E.**

The **Tanga Coral Gardens** comprise of Mwamba Wamba, Mwamba Shundo and Fungu Nyama reefs. The later reef can easily be reached as it is about eleven kilometres from Tanga. The principal features in these gardens are the **coral reefs.**

Poaching and poor conservation measures have reduced the population of turtles tremendously. This trend can be reversed if more funds and manpower are set aside as soon as possible.

Further south there are the **Dar es Salaam Coral Gardens.** Reefs of interest can be found near Mbudya and Sinda islands. The major attractions include **coconut crab,** and **limestone islands.**

Latham Island Reserve is further away, being about seventy four kilometres from Dar es Salaam. This distance gives it some protection from evercrowding. It is the centre of **nesting sea** birds and **green turtles,** but there are also fine surrounding reefs.

The **Mafia Island — Rufiji Delta** may include reefs both to the north and south of Mafia as well as a portion of the Rufiji Delta. There are different habitats ranging from fresh to brackish water, from inshore to offshore reef. The principal features in the area include **dugong, crocodile, mangrove, delta, estuary, coral reefs** and **turtles.** With proper planning, this proposed marine park could probably match some of the finest marine parks of the world.

Lastly, there is the Kilwa Reserve, known to be one of the last remaining areas where the **dugong** *(Dugong dugon)* is still relatively abundant, yet receives very little or no protection at all.

With proper conservation measures, the dugong can still exist along with turtle and other marine life.

Along with this, there is an urgent need to conserve the **mangrove communities.** Mangrove trees and shrubs are characterised by adaptations to **loose** and **wet soils, saline conditions** and **periodical tidal submergence.** They are a major feature of many coastal areas in the tropics. Yet, due to unplanned land use, today mangrove forest communities occupy less than 25% of the tropical coastline. A number of things have contributed to the present status: Unchecked firewood gathering, herbicide pollution, uncontrolled farming practices, opening up of salt pans, unplanned urban and tourist development are some of the contributing factors.

In Tanzania, like in many developing countries, mangrove ecosystems have long been neglected and very much abused and until recently, only little understood. However, despite all these short-comings, mangroves have many uses and values.

Harvesting of wood on a commercial scale is one of the many uses and values from this complex ecosystem. The direct products include construction material, fuel and charcoal wood, pulp wood, poles, fish poisons and medicines.

Even salt production can be done in mangrove areas. This is achieved by constructing salt basins; and during high tide, sea water is let in the basins and allowed to evaporate. After 3-6 days, salt crystals can be scrapped off — ready for consumption.

Of most interest is the interaction among the three communities — **coral reef, mangrove** and **sea grass.** All the three community types exhibit considerable faunal overlap, especially fishes. The presence of sea grass beds enhances nearby reef-fish biomass because of the foraging grounds these communities provide to complement the shelter provided by the reefs. Fishes migrate among all the three communities to **feed, seek shelter** or **spawn.** Hence it is obvious that anything that adversely affects one of these communities may ultimately affect the others.

Apart from what has been said, mangroves provide an important habitat for many other kinds of animal life. They are often the nesting areas for spectacular and interesting birds that can be of great attraction and value in tourism. They are also the habitat for many rare species like manatee and dugong.

Mangrove forests are found along the coast of Tanzania mainland and the islands. There are about 80,000 ha in the Mainland and about 20,000 ha in the Islands. Laws should be enforced to prevent their total elimination.

The mangrove forests appear to have the potential to serve as efficient natural sewage treatment plants due to their ability to absorb and transform large inputs of organic material. Over and above, they reduce coastal erosion, flooding and storm surge; dampening waves and high winds generated by tropical and sub-tropical storms; and perhaps lessening the ravages of tidal waves in seismically active areas.

The issue on Marine National Parks therefore defies words in description. The *first World Conference on National Parks, Seattle, 1962 resolved thus:......* "*Whereas it is recognised that the oceans and their teeming life are subject to the same dangers of human interference and destruction as the land, that the sea and land are ecologically inter-dependent and indivisible, that population pressures will cause man to turn to the sea, and especially to the underwater scene, for recreation and spiritual refreshment, and that the preservation of unspoiled marine habitat is urgently needed for ethical and aesthetic reasons, for the protection of rare species, for the replenishment of stocks of valuable food species, and for the provision of undisturbed areas of scientific research. The First World Conference on National Parks invites the Government of all those countries having marine frontiers, and other appropriate agencies, to examine as a matter of urgency the possibility of creating marine parks or reserves to defend underwater areas of special significance from all forms of human interference; and further recommends the extension of existing national parks and equivalent reserves with shorelines, into the water to 10 fathom depth or the territorial limit or some other appropriate off-shore boundary*".

SELOUS WILDLIFE RESERVE

SUMMARY

Establishment:	1922
Area:	55,000 Sq. km.
Location:	Situated between latitudes 7° 15′ and 10° 15′ S and between longitudes 36° 00′ and 38° 45′ E.
Principal features:	Rivers, hills, forest, Tanzania — Zambia Railway line.
Altitude:	Ranges from 110 to 1,250m above sea level.
Major attractions:	High concentration of various wild animals, miombo woodland, Rufiji river.
Best time to visit:	June to October.
Facilities:	Accommodation is provided at: Stieglers Gorge, Selous Safari Camp, Mbuyu Safari Camp and Rufiji River Camp; boats, vehicles at the camps, guides and airstrips.

SELOUS WILDLIFE RESERVE

The Reserve

THE Selous Wildlife Reserve, in southern Tanzania, is one of the largest wildlife areas left in the world. It is almost the same size as Ireland and nearly four times the area of the Serengeti. The reserve, established in 1922, has a total area of 55,000 sq. km It is situated between **latitudes 7° 15′** and **10° 15′ S** and between **longitudes 36° 00′** and **38° 45′ E.** Altitudes range from 110 to 1,250 metres above sea level.

And just like other regions in Tanzania, the reserve has two rainy seasons: November to January is the period for short rains while long rains begin in February and end in May. The best time to visit this area therefore is between June and October when roads are passable, the weather is cool and less humid and the animals can be seen easily.

Nearly three quarters of the vegetation in the reserve is dominated by the **Miombo** woodland *(Brachystegia spp)*. The other principal features include marshes, savannah, open plains, bushes, shrubs and thickets. The mighty Rufiji River flows through the area. Thus the Selous ecosystem is rich and diverse. It, for instance contains more than 2,000 species of plant and over 30 species of animals. Once you are in the Selous, you are in the 'bush' as it has existed for thousands of years.

The Selous Wildlife Reserve is divided into four sectors. These are: Northern, Southern, Eastern and Western sectors. The major activity is tourist hunting which is confined in Southern, Eastern and Western sectors. Animal viewing, boating, fishing and camping are restricted to the Northern sector which borders with Mikumi National Park. It is in this sector that walking safaris — accompanied by an armed ranger — can be arranged at each of the four camps.

The Selous may be reached in three different ways: by road, air or Tazara railway (Tanzania-Zambia Railway). Visitors from Dar es Salaam may either go through the Kibiti-Mkongo road to Rufiji River Camp or may go through Morogoro-Matombo-Kisaki to Stiegler's Gorge Lodge. Those intending to go by train, have to disembark at Fuga Station where they can be picked by waiting vehicles from different camps.

This, however, will have to be arranged well in advance with the camp the visitor intends to stay. The other method of travel is by air. Charter planes can land at any of the camps as each has an airstrip. Visitors are then picked by vehicles which would normally wait at a particular airstrip. The management and administrative centre of the Selous Wildlife Reserve is at Matambwe. At this centre, there are Game Wardens and Rangers and other people who have specialised in different fields. These people have been entrusted with the survival of this unique heritage.

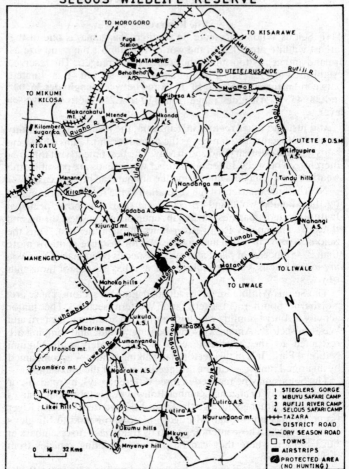

There is a simple stone slab near the Beho Beho River. The engraving on the slab is ' Capt. F.G. Selous, DSO, 25th Royal Fusiliers, Killed in action 4.1.17'. It is to this man that the park is named. This man was a naturalist, explorer and hunter. He was shot dead while scouting for the allies during the First World War.

Major Attractions

It is unquestionably true that the Selous Wildlife Reserve, like the Ngorongoro- Serengeti complex, is the only other last **stronghold of wild** animals in the world. The area is vast, but it contains such an amazing concentration of large mammals that only the Serengeti ecosystem can match it. Nevertheless it outnumbers Ngorongoro-Serengeti in some species of animals and plants. For instance the reserve boasts of over 120,000 elephants, over 160,000 buffaloes, about 2,000 rhinos', to mention but a few examples. The other animals include zebra, impala, wildebeest, waterbuck, warthog, kudu, giraffe, lion, leopard and others.

Furthermore records show that there are over 350 species of birds in the reserve, and more than 2,000 species of plants. For study and research purposes, therefore, the reserve is the best 'natural laboratory' in the world.

The leopard, with its superbly proportioned body and handsome spotted coat, is one of the most beautiful of the world's Big Cats, perfectly adapted to hunt and survive in a variety of habitats.

The **Miombo** woodland with its open canopies and groundstorey vegetation is another attraction of its own kind. The habitat is ideal for different species of animals. Perhaps, the only snag is the presence of tse tse fly, a common characteristic in the **Miombo** woodland. Nevertheless, it is part of the ecosystem operating in the area. Some species of tse tse fly such as *Glossina swynnertoni* and *Glossina pallidipes* are found in Tarangire, Lake Manyara and Selous parks. But according to research findings from the Serengeti Wildlife

Research Institute, there have been very few cases of sleeping sickness. Visitors to the various parks therefore do not have to worry much but they may carry with them a repellent that may help to protect them from the biting tse tse fly.

The mighty **Rufiji River** (with its tributaries, the Great Ruaha, Kilombero and Luwegu) flows through the reserve and it almost bisects the Selous in two halves. It makes up East Africa's largest basin draining an area of over 175, 360 sq. km. The river has an unbelievably high number of hippo schools and crocodiles which can be encountered as one sails along the river. The doum palms, the fish eagles, with their beautiful sound, the animals coming to quench their thirst while others come to wallow and play on the banks of the river, have become the centre of attraction.

In parks like Gombe Stream, Mahale and Selous, visitors are allowed to explore the wilderness on foot. Here, an armed Park Ranger is leading a group of visitors who are eager to learn about wildlife in one of the "natural laboratories". Admittedly, this is conservation in perspective.

Boating and fishing are done in this river. It is the two camps — Rufiji River and Mbuyu Safari Camps — which conduct such trips. **Walking safaris** are conducted in all the four camps. For visitors, this is perhaps a good chance to explore in its true perspective, the African wilderness. Visitors are allowed to walk at their own pace while at the same time they try to identify plants, birds, animals, rocks, soil types and so forth. In view of this, for the would-be walker, an elephant pretending to charge may send one's "adrenalin pitch" high. But it is such incidents which offer a visitor some of the best safari experience in Africa. These safaris make Selous more special than the other parks. Due to its sheer size, and the protection that it has been afforded, Selous will remain Selous for ever: It is a Reserve within a Reserve.

Facilities

There are four camps in Selous Wildlife Reserve. These are: Rufiji River, Mbuyu Safari, Selous and Stieglers Gorge. Rufiji River Camp is about 250 km. from Dar es Salaam via the Kibiti-Mkongo road. It takes about six hours to get there. A drive through this road is very fascinating indeed because one passes through coconut farms interspersed with Mango trees, cassava, pineapples, pawpaw farms and so forth.

The road is bitumenised all the way to Kibiti — about 150 km. from Dar es Salaam. Rufiji River Camp, opened in 1974, is managed by the Tanzania Safari Tours based in Dar es Salaam. It has ten double-room tents, but during the peak season it is capable of accommodating up to 30 people. There is a dining room, bar and showers. The camp also has three boats and three Landrovers for safari.

It has fishing equipment such as fishing hooks, rods etc. An airstrip to cater for visitors arriving by charter plane is close by. The Camp has Radio Call communication. The Mbuyu Safari Camp is only 30 km. from Rufiji River Camp. It has 15 double-room tents and offers luxury accommodation with electric lights and sisal mats. The tents are spacious and sheltered by **makuti** roofs. There is a verandah on each tent where one can sit and enjoy the peaceful atmosphere of the Selous.

All tents have showers, flush toilets, beds, luggage racks, clothes hanging facilities, mosquito netting and zipped in ground sheets. The bar and dining room are built under a huge baobab tree, thus the word **Mbuyu** meaning baobab in Kiswahili. The Camp has boats and landrovers for safari. It has fishing gear and Radio Call communication. Walking safaris are conducted. Like Rufiji River Camp, Mbuyu Safari Camp is built on the bank overlooking the mighty Rufiji River. In view of this, animals coming to drink water can easily be viewed from the camp.

There is an airstrip which serves the camp. The Mbuyu Camp is managed by the Hotel and Tours Management Limited whose Headquarters is in Dar es Salaam. The Selous Safari Camp is about 40 km. from Mbuyu Safari Camp. It is situated north of Rufiji River. Accommodation is provided in separate units with shower, toilet and face basin to the rear of each. There is a central unit for dining, bar and lounge facilities.

The Stieglers Gorge Safari Camp, was built in 1977 for Norwegian scientists and engineers who were working in the area; it is comfortable. Sleeping units are in separate cabins, each with a bathroom with hot and cold showers, toilet and hanging space.

101

Reception, dining, lounge and bar facilities are provided in a central area, which has an open verandah to one side with panoramic views of the countryside and adjacent watering hole. This luxurious camp has Radio Call communication and an airstrip.

The Gorge was the site where a German explorer, Stiegler, was killed by an elephant in 1907. The Selous Wildlife Reserve therefore has most of the essential equipment to cater for visitors. Indeed, a safari to this unequalled reserve can be made with a difference. Provided arrangements are made well in advance, visitors have nothing to worry about.

PROBLEMS OF TANZANIA NATIONAL PARKS

THERE are several problems facing the Tanzania National Parks. The main ones being **poaching and fire.**

In developing countries where there is a high population living at subsistence level, poaching is a common feature. Here, two poachers are celebrating their kill quietly, well aware that if Park Rangers catch them, they will be in trouble.

Poaching differs from park to park, and often even from one part to another part of the same park. There is, for instance, more poaching in the western than in the eastern Serengeti. Poaching in Manyara and Tarangire National Parks is moderate. Most poachers hunt for meat and a smaller number do kill animals for horns, ivory and skins. For meat, the most affected animals include: wildebeest, zebra, buffalo and even eland; while for horns, ivory and skins the major animals concerned are rhino, elephant and leopard. And in parks like Katavi, poachers may also go for crocodiles as their skins are quite valuable.

Different types of weapons are used during poaching; **steel wires (snares), muzzle loading muskets, shotguns and occasionally high velocity rifles** are some of the weapons used. Poaching of fish is also another problem in parks with rivers or lakes as fishing is not allowed inside the park. Most fires occurring in the parks are caused by poachers, honey gatherers or pastoralists. Sometimes, fires can be caused by visitors into the park during their tours. In large parks like the Serengeti and Ruaha, fire might continue to burn for days and sometimes for weeks before it is put off.

Fire is an important management tool. But uncontrolled fires have — most often — been harmful to the parks.

If the fire is very strong, it may cause serious damage to the vegetation and soil. In the process, much browse vegetation on which animals depend for their livelihood is destroyed; worse still, slow moving animals like tortoise, chameleon, insects and other organisms in and on the ground get killed.

AN ELDER'S IDEAS ON PARKS

FROM Arusha to Musoma by bus via the Ngorongoro and Serengeti National Parks, I shared a seat with an old man who liked his talk — and I liked it too. It was perhaps not original in substance, for he was explaining to me the people's attitude on Serengeti National Park and other wildlife areas in general. In the phrases there was nothing which would have surprised another man; yet the exactness and direction of the words seized my attention.

I reflected then, as I have done on several occasions of the sort, upon the clarity with which a man of ordinary intellectual claims can present his knowledge and convictions. The old man was very critical on the motives of setting aside some areas as National Parks and Game Reserves. He did not, for instance, see any reason as to why people should not be allowed to hunt freely in these areas as they used to do since time immemorial. He felt that people have been robbed of their land for grazing and even for settlement. In the final analysis he concluded that he was not in favour of these areas.

The fact that the old man did not see the importance of National Parks and Game Reserves hurt me most. He was not aware that the young man he was talking to was fairly knowledgeable about these Natural Laboratories. In the course of the conversation I interrupted the old man and decided to tell him the whole story: Look here "Mzee", I began, the modern idea of National Parks was born at a historic camp in Yellowstone, USA. The first National Park in the world, the Yellowstone National Park, was declared in 1872. This is not the only park "Mzee" for many other parks followed; first, in the United States and later in other countries. When the United States Government declared the Yellowstone Park it emphasized that it should be a pleasuring ground for people. A National Park therefore is first and foremost a place for the enjoyment and recreation of people. This principle was accepted internationally at a conference held in London in 1933.

"Do you have to have a conference on Natural Resources", the old man interrupted. Yes Mzee, it was that meeting which coined and gave universal significance to the expression "National Park" to donate "any area expressly reserved, acquired, controlled or managed primarily for recreation, preservation and conservation of the natural environment, historical or archaeological sites". The parks in East Africa have only been established since the First World War (Serengeti, Ngorongoro 1921) and it is true to say that in all three East African countries there was considerable opposition to the consolidation of parks soon after the Second World War because very few people understood what they were. You might be one of them, I told the old man. He looked at me and said: "Perhaps I was not born by then".

Most people thought of the National Parks, I continued my story, as being just an excuse to deny the people use of the land. They forget that very often the land in anycase is quite unsuitable for farming, either due to tse-tse fly, lack of water or poor soils and thus National Parks are the best form of land use for the reserves. The people of various countries in Africa and the world at large, should gain full benefit from the Parks and Game Reserves established in their countries. The Safari Lodges, camps, trucks and other facilities are open to everybody regardless of race, colour or creed.

In Uganda, Kenya and Tanzania provision has been made for all types of parties and special camps for schools and other organized parties have been built offering accommodation at very low prices. The Parks and Game Reserves are a very good place for a rest and a holiday amidst the great beauties of nature and away from the hustle and bustle of the cities. They are places to relax and forget your troubles. **To provide places for recreation for the people** is one of the objectives of these areas.

Visitors admiring antelopes. The economic gains are great. No wonder the future for the tourism industry in Tanzania looks bright indeed.

To preserve the animals and their environment is another objective of no less importance. There used to be many more wild animals in Africa than there are today. Unless positive action is taken to preserve them, they will soon disappear altogether.

It is not only uncontrolled hunting that is destorying the animals; a number of other factors come into play: population explosion, better farming methods, unnecessary fires and so on, can wipe out a large population of animals. If we want to conserve animals we must conserve their habitats first.

Even if the animals themselves are not destroyed these various activities use the land which was at one time occupied by animals; you obviously cannot have wild animals wandering over a modern farm.

The animals are worth preserving for themselves and we should give them some place in which they can lead their lives undisturbed. Many visitors are surprised to see that these creatures are not frightened of people in a National Park. They seem to have learnt to accept each other. The park teaches us the lesson of kindness to animals and it is an important lesson for all people to learn.

If we allow these animals to be destroyed, future generations will know nothing of all this and something important will have been lost. We have in Africa, and East Africa in particular, a very remarkable collection of wild animals. Nowhere else in the world can you see such a variety of animals, and in such large concentrations. It is, in fact, unique in Tanzania!

Tanzania offers immense concentrations of plain animals. Uganda has vast herds of elephant, buffalo and large numbers of hippo. Kenya has also vast herds of plain animals and elephant to name only a few of the many attractions. This is one of the unique offerings which Africa can make for the benefit of the whole world.

People sometimes ask why animals cannot be preserved on some quite small area of land or zoos. In order to lead their natural life the animals need room to move and obtain sufficient food; there must be enough of them to allow for natural breeding. Each Park or Reserve must therefore be a sound ecological unit. In this way they are much the same as people; for all races have rules which forbid marriage between close relations, or betweeen members of the same clans. If we did not have these rules, the human race would have perished, as a result of inbreeding.

It is the same with the animals. You can therefore look at the various herds of antelope as if they were so many different clans that make it easier to understand why a National Park must be larger. You enjoy watching the animals far more if you know that they are healthy and leading entirely natural lives. This therefore is the second reason for establishing Parks and Reserves: **the protection of the animals in their natural environment.**

The third reason for having Parks and Reserves is the **economic aspect.** East Africa now receives thousands of visitors annually from all over the world. Thus tourism in East African countries, particularly Tanzania which has limited resources, such as mineral wealth, can be considered as a major industry comparable to textile manufacture. Indeed, it could be East Africa's substitute for oil if well developed and managed.

The existence of wild animals depends — to a large extent — on proper management of the environment. These animals are enjoying a healthy life in their natural habitat.

It is reckoned that each tourist spends over US$ 1,000. This money is generated in respect of entry fees, transport and accommodation. The money so generated is not only spent on parks' activities but also on other government expenditures. However, a considerable amount of money is required to keep the Parks going. The overheads are great; the maintenance of tracks and buildings, suppression of poaching and so on, require a lot of money. A National Park is a public service to the people of the country; and as a public service it has to be paid for. Money is therefore provided by the government for that matter, in a form of subvention.

There is another important point about visitors from overseas and it is this one that few people understand at all. They visit Tanzania and Africa in general to see the game, but they also see the people of those countries. They meet the residents and talk to them. When they go home, these visitors probably become interested in the countries they have visited. They form the beginning of an informed world public opinion, perhaps sympathetic and interested in the affairs of Africa.

We can say one more thing on this subject, I told the old man. The National Parks and the preservation of wildlife and nature, **is part of our culture, not only from the aesthetic point of view, but also from the**

research and management angle. The study of the African animals is a comparatively new science. Research units are now being set up in National Parks with a view to a detailed study of the fauna and flora of certain areas. This relates to applied and pure research.

The Research Units set up in our National Parks and Game Reserves are in contact with some universities in the world and have the services of some of the finest brains in the world dealing with ecological problems. In years to come we hope the world will judge Africa by its culture. The National Parks have something to show the whole world; it is therefore the duty of every citizen to support them and ensure for their survival.

Closely related to this is the ethical obligation. What this means is illustrated by a quotation from the Arusha manifesto. *"The survival of our wildlife is a matter of grave concern to all of us in Africa. These wild creatures amid the wild places they inhabit are not only important as a source of wonder and inspiration but are an integral part of our natural resources and of our future livelihood and well-being.*

In accepting the trusteeship of our wildlife we solemnly declare that we will do everything in our power to make sure that our children's grand children will be able to enjoy this rich and precious inheritance. The conservation of wildlife and wild places calls for specialist knowledge, trained manpower and money and we look to other nations to co-operate in this important task — the success or failure of which not only affects the continent of Africa but the rest of the world as well"

We were now passing through the Ikizu settlement and the old man seemed to be impressed with my talk. I hesitated to continue with the discussion for we were approaching our destination. Before we parted at the Musoma bus stand the old man himself summarised the story and said: *"Oh what a beautiful surprise! Tanzania....... a country of striking differences — geographically, historically and culturally. Nestled between the Indian Ocean and Lake Tanganyika, Tanzania has more to offer to the world than other African countries. Incredible natural beauty. A combination of the old and the new. Like medieval towns and ultramodern hotels. As well as an endless variety of sports, beaches, national parks, wildlife reserves and festivals. Tanzania is still one of the best values in the world"* As he got out of the bus, the old man put his mouth in the form of a smile, and put it back without smiling and said: "Yes young man, you seem to know your stuff, now I have got the message"

Lastly, when he was boarding a minibus to Majita, I jokingly asked him to take care of the animals. At this juncture he laughed and replied — take care too chap!

THE NATIONAL PARKS REGULATIONS

WHILE you are in the park, it is very important to observe the Parks' Regulations. These regulations are so important that if violated, "the warden may order any person to leave the Park, if in his opinion, the presence of such a person in the Park is or would be detrimental to the Park". If this happens, the whole safari may turn out to be an unforgettable and costly experience.

The eye-catching sight in the parks will certainly give you the thrill of a lifetime provided you remember the following points.-

— A permit is required for entrance into the park. This is obtainable at the gate of each respective park.

— No person is allowed to stay, camp or be in any camping site for any period, between the hours of 7 p.m. and 7 a.m. otherwise than on payment of the prescribed fee.

— Park management has the right to close any road in the park. Please do not attempt to travel on such portion of the road.

— This is the wild animal's land. Entrance to the park therefore should be in a motor vehicle having four or more wheels. At present the only exception is at Gombe Stream, Mahale, Rubondo Island and Mount Kilimanjaro National Parks where walking safaris are conducted.

— Parks open at 6 a.m. and entrance before this time is prohibited. Likewise, closure time is at 7 p.m. and if this time is exceeded one would be contravening this regulation.

— With the exception of Gombe Stream, Mahale, Rubondo Island and Mount Kilimanjaro National Parks, no person is allowed to be beyond 25 metres from a motor vehicle. This has been taken as a precaution against dangerous animals.

— The slower you drive the more you will see. It is forbidden to exceed a speed of 50 kilometres per hour in a motor vehicle within the Park.

TANZANIA WILDLIFE

THE Wildlife in Tanzania is so diverse that it is almost impossible to give a fair account on this wonderful heritage. A variety of animals can be encountered in different parts of the country due to different types of habitat. These ecologic niches are so important that they influence the carrying capacity; without them there would be no food and escape cover — and in the final analysis there would actually be no animals. In most parts of the world — especially in developing countries — wildlife resources are being misused or destroyed through land clearing, drainage, and overgrazing. The story of the destruction and conservation of wild animals in North America, for instance, is a dramatic one that has often been told. It features the work of many men and organisations, and the conflict between selfish interests and those from whom the future of their country meant more than the prospect of immediate gain.

Yet, even then, Tanzania is still striving to preserve and conserve this precious heritage in its natural habitat for all mankind to marvel at. Therefore it is not accidental to find many animals scattered across the country as shown on the following page.

THE NATIONAL PARKS ORDINANCE

(Cap. 412)
REGULATIONS

Made under Section 18
THE NATIONAL PARKS (AMENDMENT) REGULATIONS, 1986

FIRST SCHEDULE

FEES for the period commencing at the time of arrival and ending after twenty-four hours on the following day or part of such period and for each following period of twenty-four hours or part   thereof spent in the Parks:-

A. Permit for the entry of each person:-

	Resident	Non-Resident
	Shs. Cts.	US $
(i) of or above the age of 16 years	50 00	10
(ii) between the age of 3 years and 16 years	20 00	5
(iii) of or below the age of 3 years	Free	Free

B. Permit for each motor vehicle

	Tanzanian	Foreign
	Shs. Cts.	US $
(i) tare weight up to 2,000 kg	200 00	30
(ii) tare weight over 2,000 kg.	2500 00	120

A foreign motor vehicle is any vehicle coming from outside Tanzania and bearing foreign registration

(iii) Long term permit for residents' vehicle:-

(1) tare weight up to 2000 kg.

per annum or prorata or quarterly basis   Shs.   9000/-

(2) tare weight over 2000 kg per annum or
prorata or quarterly basis   Shs. 24000/-

C. Permit for camping in any one period of twenty-four hours or part thereof:-

114

	Resident	Non-Resident
	Shs. Cts.	US $

(i) On established camping sites:-

Each person above the age of 16 years	50 00	6
Each person between 3 and 16 years of age	20 00	3

(ii) In places other than established|camping sites:-

	Residents	Non-Residents
	Shs. Cts.	US $
Eacn person of or above the age of 16 years	100 00	12
Each person between 3 and 16 years of age	20 00	3
Each person of or under the age of 3 years	Free	Free

D. Permit for the landing of aircrafts

	Private Shs. Cts.	Commercial Shs. Cts.
(i) Locally Registered		
1. Up to 6 seater	200 00	400 .00
2. 7 - 18 Seater	600 00	1200 00
3. Over 18 Seater	1500 00	3000 00
(ii) Foreign Registered		
1. Up to 6 Seater	US$ 30	US$ 200
2. 7 - 18 Seater	90	400
3. Over 18 Seater	150	600

	Resident	Non-Resident
E. Guide Fees:-		
(i) The fees for the service of an official guide are as follows:-	50 00	10
(ii) The fees for the service of an official guide who accompanies the tourist outside his normal station are as follows:	150 00	15

F.   Hotel Concession Fees:—
A fee of 10% per bed night shall be payable by the owner or proprietor of a hotel or lodge in respect of each person who lodges or stays in such a hotel or lodge.

SECOND SCHEDULE

A.   Cinematography/Video/Film

Number of persons (including artists, technicians or administrative staff) making or participating in the making of film.

1-10 persons		
First Week	—	800 US $
Second Week	—	600 US $
Third Week	—	400 US $
For each subsequent week	—	200 US $
11-20 persons		
First Week	—	1600 US$
Second Week	—	1300 US $
Third Week	—	1000 US $
For each subsequent week	—	600 US $
More than 20 persons		
First Week	—	2600 US $
Second Week	—	2000 US $
Third Week	—	1300 US $
For each subsequent week	—	600 US $

For every week or part of it during which film is being taken.

(Each National Park appearing in the film will receive a copy of each such film irrespective of the charge above which are inclusive of entry fees.)

- It is an offence to sound a motor horn within the Park.

- It is the desire of the Parks' management not to interfere with the environment. In view of this, no person shall be allowed to remove from the Park any animal or vegetation, any object of geological, prehistoric, archaeological, historical or other scientific interest.

- It is illegal to introduce any animal or vegetation into the Park.

- Animals too need peace. No person while within the Park, shall molest, provoke, feed or disturb any animal.

- Fire is used in the Park as a management tool. However, no person while within the Park shall light a fire; leave any fire which has been lighted, unextinguished; discard any burning object.

- It is not allowed to discard any refuse or litter while within the Park.

- Aircrafts can land in the park on specified airfields. Permission to land has to be sought from the Director or Warden.

- Except for the purpose of landing or taking off or in an emergency, no person within the Park, is allowed to fly any aircraft at an altitude of less than 460 metres above the ground.

- The fees specified in the First and Second Schedules to these Regulations shall be paid for:

- entry permit;
- vehicle permit
- landing of aircrafts permit;
- camping permit;
- guide service;
- hotel concession;
- cinematography, video and film.

Assist the Park Authority to manage the Park to the required standards by abiding to the National Parks Regulations.

ANIMALS \ PARK	SERENGETI	MANYARA	TARANGIRE	ARUSHA	K'NJARO	MIKUMI	RUAHA	KATAVI	GOMBE	MAHALE	RUBONDO	UZUNGWA	NGO'RO	SELOUS
1. Aardvark	•		•			•	•	•				•	•	
2. Baboon	•	•	•	•	•	•	•	•	•	•	•	•	•	•
3. Bat-eared Fox	•	•	•			•	•	•				•	•	•
4. Black and White Colobus Monkey	•,			•	•				•		•			•
5. Blue Monkey	•	•	•	•	•	•	•	•	•	•		•	•	•
6. Buffalo	•	•	•	•	•	•	•	•	•	•		•	•	•
7. Bush Pig	•	•	•	•	•	•	•	•	•	•	•	•	•	•
8. Bush buck	•	•	•	•	•	•	•	•	＼	•		•	•	•
9. Civet	•	•	•		•	•	•	•		•			•	•
10. Chimpanzee									•	•				
11. Cheetah	•	•	•			•	•	•				•	•	•
12. Dik Dik	•	•	•,	•		•	•	•		•	•	•	•	•
13. Duiker	•	•	•	•	•	•	•	•	•	•		•	•	•
14. Eland	•		•		•	•	•	•		•		•	•	•
15. Elephant	•	•	•	•	•	•	•	•		•	•	•	•	•
16. Genet	•	•	•	•	•	•	•	•		•		•	•	•
17. Gerenuk	•	•	•			•	•	•		•		•	•	•
18. Giraffe	•	•	•	•	•	•	•	•		•	•	•	•	•
19. Grants Gazelle	•	•	•	•		•	•	•		•		•	•	•
20. Grysbok (sharpe's)									•					•
21. Greater Kudu	•					•								•
22. Hartebeest	•	•	•			•	•	•		•		•	•	•
23. Hippo	•	•	•	•		•	•	•		•	•	•	•	•
24. Honey Badger	•			•		•	•	•		•			•	•
25. Hyrax	•	•	•	•	•	•	•	•	•	•	•	•	•	•
26. Hyena	•	•	•			•	•	•		?		•	•	•
27. Impala	•	•	•	•		•	•	•		•		•	•	•
28. Jackal	•	•	•	•	•	•	•	•		•		•	•	•
29. Klipspringer	•	•	•			•	•	•		•		•	•	•
30. Leopard	•	•	•	•	•	•	•	•	•	•		•	•	•
31. Lesser Kudu	•		•				•							•
32. Lion	•	•	•			•	•	•		•		•	•	•
33. Mongoose	•	•	•			•	•	•		•		•	•	•
34. Oryx			•				•	•				•	•	•
35. Oribi	•	•	•			•	•	•					•	•
36. Red Colobus Monkey							•	•		•				
37. Reedbuck	•	•	•	•	•	•	•	•		•		•	•	•
38. Roan Antelope	•		•			•	•	•				•	•	•
39. Rhino	•	•	•	•		•	•	•		•	•	•	•	•
40. Sable Antelope	•		•			•	•	•				•	•	•
41. Sanje Mangabey										:		•		
42. Serval	•	•	•	•	•	•	•	•		•		•	•	•
43. Sitatunga										•				•
44. Steenbok	•					•	•	•		•				•
45. Squirrel	•	•	•	•	•	•	•	•	•	•	•	•	•	•,
46. Suni	•	•	•	•	•	•	•	•		•		•	•	•
47. Sykes Monkey								•				•		
48. Topi	•					•		•				•		
49. Thomson's Gazelle	•	•	?			•	•					•		
50. Warthog	•	•	•	•	•	•	•	•	•	•	•	•	•	•
51. Waterbuck	•	•	•	•	•	•	•	•	•	•	•	•	•	•
52. Wildebeest	•	•	•	•		•	•	•		•		•	•	•
53. Wild Dog	•						•						•	•
54. Vervet Monkey	•		•	•	•	•	•	•	•	•		•	•	•
55. Zebra	•	•	•		•	•	•			•		•	•	•
56. Zorilla	•					•	•	•		•			•	•

K'NJARO = Kilimanjaro   **NGO'RO = Ngorongoro**

DISTANCES

THE following Distance-Time Charts are intended to guide visitors to various places, by way of distance to be covered and time taken between two points. The distance is in kilometres while the time is in hours. Visitors are cautioned that the distance and the time have been approximated taking into consideration the nature of the road between the points. The Chart is read by taking two points: where they meet, at right angle, that is the distance. The corresponding number is the time.

Taking an example; the distance from Arusha to Lobo is 405 km and the time taken — on a normal drive — would be about 7¼ hours, by minibus. Admittedly, where the distance and timing are not shown, it means that the time taken would be impracticable for a normal safari.

DISTANCE—TIME CHART NO. 1

	Arusha	Time	Tarangire	Time	Manyara	Time	Ngorongoro	Time	Ndutu Camp	Time	Seronera	Time	Fort Ikoma	Time	Musoma	Time	Mwanza	Time	Lobo	Time	Keekorok	Time
Tarangire	120	2																				
Manyara	130	2½	95	1¼																		
Ngorongoro	190	3½	155	2¼	60	1																
Ndutu Camp	280	4¾	245	3½	150	2¼	90	1¼														
Seronera	335	6	300	4¼	205	3	145	2½	80	1¼												
Fort Ikoma	390	6½	335	5¾	260	4½	200	3½	135	2¼	55	1										
Musoma	670	10¾	550	8½	450	7	390	6	300	4¾	220	3½	165	2½								
Mwanza	750	12	630	9¼	530	8¼	770	7½	380	6¼	300	5	355	6	240	3½						
Lobo	405	7½	385	6¼	285	4¾	225	3¾	160	2½	80	1¼	100	1½	265	4½	380	6¼				
Keekorok	570	9¾	450	7¼	350	6	290	4¾	225	3¾	145	2½	165	2½	330	5¾	455	7½	65	1¼		
Nairobi	280	4	400	7	410	7	470	7½	490	8	615		670	10¾	—	—	—	—	330	5¾	265	3½

DISTANCE — TIME CHART NO. 2

Each cell shows distance (km) and time (hours).

	Arusha (time)	Momella (time)	Moshi (time)	Marangu (time)	Kilaguni (time)	Ngulia (time)	Voi Lodge (time)	Mombasa (time)	Namanga (time)	Amboseli (time)
Momella	50 / 1									
Moshi	80 / 1¼	80 / 1¼								
Marangu	120 / 2	120 / 2	40 / 1							
Kilaguni	255 / 3½	255 / 3½	175 / 2½	135 / 2						
Ngulia	260 / 3½	260 / 3½	180 / 2½	140 / 2	35 / ¾					
Voi Lodge	265 / 3½	265 / 3½	185 / 2½	145 / 2	115 / 1½	90 / 1¼				
Mombasa	425 / 5	425 / 5	345 / 4	305 / 3¾	275 / 3½	240 / 3	160 / 2			
Namanga	110 / 1½	115 / 1½	190 / 2½	230 / 3	195 / 2½	230 / 3	— / —	— / —		
Amboseli	190 / 2½	195 / 2½	— / —	— / —	115 / 1½	150 / 1¾	— / —	— / —	80 / 1¼	
Nairobi	280 / 3¾	285 / 3¾	360 / 4¼	— / —	275 / 3½	290 / 3¾	335 / 4	495 / 5	170 / 2½	250 / 3½

DISTANCE—TIME CHART NO. 3

	D'Salaam	Time	Bagamoyo	Time	Morogoro	Time	Mikumi Lodge	Time	Iringa	Time
Bagamoyo	75	1¼								
Morogoro	195	2½	190	2¼						
Mikumi Lodge	295	3¼	290	3¾	215	2¾				
Iringa	510	7	505	7	315	3¾	215	2¾		
Ruaha Park Entry	695	9¾	620	8	430	5	330	5½	155	2½

DISTANCE—TIME CHART NO. 4

	D'Salaam	(Time)	Kibiti	(Time)	Mkongo	(Time)	Rufiji Camp	(Time)	Mbuyu	(Time)	Selous Camp	(Time)	Stieglers
Kibiti	150	2¾											
Mkongo	180	3¾	30	1									
Rufiji Camp	260	6¼	110	3½	80	2½							
Mbuyu	290	7¼	140	4½	110	3½	30	1					
Selous Camp	330	8¾	180	6	150	5	70	2½	40	1½			
Stieglers	380	10	230	7½	200	6½	120	4	90	3	50	1½	

NATIONAL PARKS AND
OTHER WILDLIFE AREAS

SUMMARY

1. NATIONAL PARKS

A NATIONAL park represents a particular kind of land use intended to permit the maximum appreciation of protected areas of high value because of the nature and quality of their **flora, fauna** or **landscapes.**

A national park therefore is **"any area expressly acquired and managed primarily for recreation, or preservation or conservation of the natural environment, historical or archaeological sites"**. In these areas, visitors are allowed to enter, under special conditions, for **inspirational, educational** and **recreational purposes.**

The parks have also been set aside for **future generations** as well as for both **aesthetic and** economical value.

2. CONSERVATION AREAS:

The word **conservation** (which means proper use of our natural resources) may be misleading to some people. But for our purpose here, there is only one conservation area — Ngorongoro. The area attempts to integrate in the best way, the interests and rights of the pastoral Maasai, the conservation of natural resources and tourism.

As a result the Ngorongoro Conservation Area has been zoned to include particular land use areas that are compatible with each of these interests.

Agriculture is prohibited, but Maasai activities such as livestock grazing and residence are allowed. Preservation of natural resources, research, and tourism continue in conjunction with human activities.

3. GAME/WILDLIFE RESERVES:

There are more than 15 Game and/or Wildlife Reserves, among which is the world's largest — the Selous Wildlife Reserve. Game Reserves are administered by the Game Department assisted by their respective Regional Directorates. Apart from protecting the animals and plants, Game Reserves have been set aside as limited natural resource use sites.

Therefore, some human activities can take place in the reserve, yet residence — except for reserve employees — is prohibited. Licensed professional hunting is allowed only between July and December.

The following are the Game Reserves and their areas:—

RESERVE'S NAME	AREA (SQ KM)	REGION(S) FOUND
1. Selous	55,000	Coast, Morogoro, Lindi, Mtwara and Ruvuma
2. Saadani	300	Coast
3. Rungwa	9,000	Singida
4. Kizigo	4,000	Singida
5. Moyowosi	6,000	Kigoma
6. Ugalla	5,000	Tabora/Rukwa
7. Uwanda	5,000	Rukwa
8. Maswa	2,200	Shinyanga
9. Burigi	2,200	Kagera
10. Biharamulo	1,300	Kagera
11. Rumanyika Orugundu	800	Kagera
12. Ibanda	200	Kagera
13. Umba	1,500	Tanga
14. Mkomazi	1,000	Kilimanjaro
15. Kilimanjaro	900	Kilimanjaro
16. Mount Meru	300	Arusha
17. Saa Nane Island	0.5	Mwanza

4. GAME CONTROLLED AREAS:

Approximately 50-60 Game controlled Areas exist in Tanzania. They cover about 121,655 Sq. Km. spread across the country. These areas are administered by the Game Department through Regional Directorates.

Licensed hunting for all game species is approved except for specifically designated animals. The licence can be obtained from the Director of Game Division.

Game control against crop or property is allowed. All such game control must be reported to the game officials as soon as possible.

5. FOREST RESERVES:

Forest Reserves are supervised by the Forestry Department, and in these areas human habitation is limited to reserve employees only. The purposes of setting aside Forest Reserves are many and varied. They include the following:-

(i) **Natural National Heritage and Tourism:** To the non-resident to Tanzania, the most apparent reason for conserving these forests is for their uniqueness. This is an attraction to the visitor. The Kilimanjaro forest is a good example.

(ii) **Watershed:** Providing water to the surrounding agricultural lands and fishing areas. Without it, soil erosion, followed by floods may easily occur. The area may no longer store water for release to the surrounding areas in the dry seasons. In view of these circumstances, deserts may soon follow. In this regard, the Ngorongoro highlands, the Mount Meru and Kilimanjaro forests support the argument.

(iii) **Climate:** Forests have an effect on rainfall. The larger the forest the more its effect to agriculture. They are also a major source of the Oxygen supply.

(iv) **Research:** Admittedly, forests give us a standard with which to compare the ecological changes with human activities on the natural environment.

(v) **Genetic Storehouse:** Through conservation of forests, we conserve an invaluable genetic wealth. The genetic diversity allows possibilities for the discovery and development of:-
   — medicines from plant and animal material; for example the Traditional Medicine Research Department at Muhimbili Medical Centre is involved in this field;
   — alternative sources of fuel and rubber;
   — food crops;
   — animal species important for husbandry and medical research;
   — insect species important for the control of crop pests. For instance in early 1988, Tanzania imported from Nigeria some insects — *wasps* — which were used to control pests that were attacking cassava plants;
   — predators of pests: many animal species living in the forest that feed on insects (insectivores) which are pests to man and his food crops. Birds, bats and predators of insects are examples. Total destruction of forests means the loss of many insectivorous species which are beneficial to man.

In Tanzania, forest reserves are scattered all over the country. Some of these are administered by the local governments in the regions.

Timber and animal harvesting can be done in these areas after obtaining a licence from the Directors of Forestry and Game Departments respectively. The total area under Forest Reserves is about 134,075 Sq. Km. This area includes both productive and protective areas.

CONCLUSION

TANZANIA has a total area of about 939,701 sq. km. of which 53,000 Sq. km. are inland water. At present it has 13 parks — including Ngorongoro Conservation Area and Selous — which cover a total area of 102,658 sq. km; this is about 11% of the total area of the country. Furthermore, it has 16 Game Reserves occupying 39,750 sq. km or 4% of Tanzania's area. Another 134,075 sq. km. are under the Forest Reserves; admittedly, 50-60 controlled areas with an area of about 121,655 sq. km. are scattered all over the country: These impressive statistics, show the dedication of Tanzania in wildlife conservation for all mankind to come and see. Yet, despite being so poor, in terms of economics, the country is spending more money on wildlife conservation than the United States of America!

Apart from wildlife areas, Tanzania has good beaches and marine life stretching for 800 km. from Tanga in the north to the mouth of Ruvuma River in the south. There are also beautiful landscape sceneries and historical sites both on Mainland Tanzania and the islands of Zanzibar, Pemba and Mafia.

. The other outstanding geographical features include the snow-capped Mount Kilimanjaro — the highest mountain in Africa; Lake Victoria —the world second largest; Lake Tanganyika — the second deepest in the world; and the Rift Valley. There is evidence at Olduvai Gorge that the world's oldest known man in his present form lived in this country more than 1.75 million years ago.

Hotel and/or lodge accommodation to visitors is available in the national parks and in towns. Most of these hotels/lodges are managed by the Tanzania Tourist Corporation (TTC). The State Travel Service Ltd., a subsidiary of TTC, with a number of other Tour Operators, provide package tours and excursions to tourist areas.

USEFUL INFORMATION

THE following addresses are useful to those people who are interested in knowing more about Tanzania National Parks, tourism, hunting, where to stay, air and ground transportation as well as tours.

1. ON TOURISM

— Ministry of Lands, Natural Resources and Tourism
   Box 9132 Dar es Salaam
   Tel. 21241/9 27271/7   Tlx: 41725

— The Tourism Division
   Box 9352 Dar es Salaam
   Tel: 21241/9 Tlx: 41725

— Tanzania Tourist Corporation
   Box 2485, Dar es Salaam
   Tel: 27672/3 Tlx: 41061 TTC DAR

— Zanzibar Tourist Corporation
   Box 216, Zanzibar
   Tel: 30345, 32344 Tlx: 57144

2. ON WILDLIFE

— Wildlife Division
   Box 1994 Dar es Salaam
   Tel: 27811

— College of African Wildlife Management
   Box 3031 Moshi
   Tel: 18 KIBOSHO

3. ON TANZANIA NATIONAL PARKS

— Tanzania National Parks
   AICC KILIMANJARO BLOCK
   Box 3134 Arusha
   Tel: 3471, 3181 Tlx: 42130 TANAPA TZ.

— The Chief Park Warden
     Serengeti National Park,
     Box 3134 Arusha

— The Chief Park Warden
     Lake Manyara National Park
     Box 3134 Arusha or Box 12 Mto wa Mbu

— The Senior Park Warden
     Tarangire National Park
     Box 3134, Arusha

— The Chief Park Warden
     Arusha National Park
     Box 3134, Arusha

— The Chief Park Warden
     Kilimanjaro National Park
     Box 96, Marangu Moshi
     Tel: 50 Marangu

— The Chief Park Warden
     Mikumi National Park
     Box 62, Mikumi Morogoro

— The Chief Park Warden
     Ruaha National Park
     Box 369, Iringa

— The Senior Park Warden
     Katavi National Park
     Box 89 Mpanda

— The Senior Park Warden
     Mountain Mahale National Park
     Box 1053 Kigoma

— The Park Warden Incharge
     Gombe Stream National Park
     Box 185, Kigoma

— The Park Warden Incharge
     Rubondo Island National Park
     Box 111 Geita.

— Conservator of Ngorongoro
  Goliondoi Road
  Box 776, Arusha

— The Chief Conservation Warden
  Ngorongoro Crater
  Box 776, Arusha

— The Chief Wildlife Warden
  Selous Wildlife Reserve
  Box 25295 Dar es Salaam
  Tel: 32680

4. ON HUNTING

Tanzania Wildlife Corporation
Box 1144, Arusha
Tel: 3501/2 Tlx: 42080 TAWICO

5. ON TOUR OPERATORS

— State Travel Service Limited,
  Box 1369 Arusha
  Tel: 3300, 3113/4, 3152 Tlx: 42138 TRAVEL TZ.

— Ranger Safaris Ltd.
  Box 9 Arusha
  Tel: 3074, 3867, 3023 Tlx: 42107 RANGER TZ

— Lions Safari International
  Box 999 Arusha
  Tel: 6422 Tlx: 42119 LIONS

— Simba Safaris
  Box 1207 Arusha
  Tel: 3509, 3600 Tlx: 42095 SS TOURS TZ

— Game Trails of East Africa Limited
  Box 2660 Arusha,
  Tel: 6976, 6152 Tlx: 42003 EVETTS

— Flamingo Tours of East Africa
  Box 2660 Arusha
  Tel: 6976, 6152 Tlx: 42003 EVETTS

— African Gametracks Limited
Box 535 Arusha
Tel: 3779 Tlx: 42075 MAUA TZ

— Arusha International Conference Centre,
Box 3081 Arusha
Tel: 3181, 3161 Tlx: 42121 AICC TZ

— Executive Tours
Box 6162 Arusha
Tel: 2472, 7199 Tlx: 42058

— Abercrombie and Kent (T) Ltd
Box 427 Arusha
Tel: 7803, 3181 Ext 1420 Tlx: 42005 ABKENT

— Wildersun Safaris
Box 930 Arusha
Tel: 3880 Tlx. 42126 CK TVL TZ

— State Travel Service Ltd
Box 5023 Dar es Salaam
Tel: 29291-8 Tlx: 41508 TRAVEL TZ.

WHERE TO STAY

ARUSHA

Hotel Seventy Seven
Box 1184 Arusha
Tel: 3800/6, 3820 Tlx: 42055 SEVTEL-TZ

Mount Meru Hotel
Box 877 Arusha
Tel: 2711, 2728 Tlx: 42065 MERHT TZ

Mount Meru Game Lodge Ltd
Box 427 Arusha.
Tel. Usa River 43 Tlx. 42005 ABKENT

Ngaresero Mountain Lodge
Box 425 Arusha
Tel: 3529 or 38 Usa River Tlx: 42047 MMARS

Gibbs Farm
Box 1501 Karatu
Tel: 25 Karatu

New Safari Hotel
Box 303 Arusha
Tel: 3261/2

New Arusha Hotel
Box 88 Arusha
Tel: 3241/2, 3727 Tlx: 42034

Hotel Equator
Box 3002 Arusha
Tel: 3127 Tlx: 42034

Hotel Arusha By Night
Box 360 Arusha
Tel: 2836

Hotel Tanzanite
Box 3063 Arusha
Tel: 32 Usa River Tlx: 42116 SAFARI

Momela Lodge
Box 418 Arusha
Tel: 3798, 3038

Lake Manyara Hotel
Box 3100 Arusha
Tel: 10, 11 MTO WA MBU Tlx: 42037 UTALII TZ

Ngorongoro Wildlife Lodge
Box 3100
Tel: 15 Ngorongoro Tlx: 42037 UTALII -TZ

Ngorongoro Crater Lodge
Box 427 Arusha
Tel. 3530, 7803 Tlx. 42005 ABKENT

Seronera Wildlife Lodge
Box 3100 Arusha
Tlx: 42037 UTALII-TZ

Lobo Wildlife Lodge
Box 3100 Arusha
Tlx: 42037 UTALII - TZ

MOSHI

Moshi Hotel Ltd
Box 1819 Moshi
Tel: 3071 ·

Y.M.C.A.
Box 85 Moshi
Tel: 2362

Kibo Hotel
Box 102 Marangu, Moshi
Tel: 4 Marangu Tlx: 42095 SS TOURS TZ

Marangu Hotel
Box 40 Moshi
Tel: 11 Marangu

DAR ES SALAAM

Kilimanjaro Hotel
Box 9574 Dar es Salaam
Tel: 21281/8 Tlx: 41021

New Africa Hotel
Box 9314 Dar es Salaam
Tel: 29611/9 Tlx: 41061 TTC DAR

Kunduchi Beach Hotel
Box 9313 Dar es Salaam
Tel: 47621, 47622 Tlx: 41061 TTC DAR

Bahari Beach Hotel
Box 9312 Dar es Salaam
Tel: 47101 Tlx: 41185

Hotel Embassy
24 Garden Avenue
Box 3152 Dar es Salaam
Tel: 30006, 30035 Tlx: 41570, 41666 EMBASSY—TZ

Motel Agip
Sokoine Drive
Box 529 Dar es Salaam
Tel: 23551 Tlx: 41276 MOTAGI—TZ

SELOUS

Stieglers Gorge Safari Camp
Rubada
Box 9320 Dar es Salaam
Tel: 48724 Tlx: 41135 Rubada

Mbuyu Safari Camp
Hotel and Tours Management Ltd
Box 5350 Dar es Salaam
Tel: 31957, 32671 Tlx: 41178

Rufiji River Camp
Box 20058 Dar es Salaam

Selous Safari Camp
Box 1907 Dar es Salaam.
Tel: 68631/2/3 Tlx: 41573

MOROGORO

Morogoro Hotel
Box 1144, Morogoro
Tel: 3270/2 Tlx: 55100

Savoy Hotel
Box 35, Morogoro
Tel: 2345

Mikumi Wildlife Lodge
Box 84 Mikumi - Morogoro
Tel: 27

Mikumi Wildlife Camp
Box 64, Mikumi-Morogoro

RUAHA NATIONAL PARK (Iringa)

Msembe Camp
Box 369
Iringa

Ruaha River Camp
Box 84
Mufindi.

or

Ruaha River Camp
Valji & Alibhai
Box 786
Dar es Salaam
Tel: 20522/26537/37561

REFERENCES

INTERESTING BOOKS ON TANZANIA'S PARKS AND WILDLIFE RESERVES

Arusha National Park	— A guide by Tanzania National Parks
* Lake Manyara National Park	— A guide by Tanzania National Parks
* Lake Manyara National Park	— Master Plan, by College of African Wildlife Management, Mweka, Moshi
* Marine and Coastal Conservation in the East African Region (1984)	— By UNEP Regional Seas Report and Studies No. 39
* Marine Parks for Tanzania (1968)	— By Carleton Ray
* Mikumi National Park	— A guide by Tanzania National Parks

* Ngorongoro Conservation Area

— Annual Reports 1962 — 1967

— Booklets on First Visitor, Animals, Birds, Geology, Trees and Shrubs.

— (In Preparation) Annual Reports 1968— 1982

* Ruaha National Park	— A guide by Tanzania National Parks
* Serengeti National Park	— A guide by Tanzania National Parks
* Tarangire National Park	— A guide by Tanzania National Parks